SIMPLY SILVER,
SIMPLY GOLD

DESIGNS FOR CREATING PRECIOUS BEAD JEWELRY

NANCY ALDEN
COFOUNDER OF BEADWORKS

SIMPLY SILVER, SIMPLY GOLD

DESIGNS FOR CREATING PRECIOUS BEAD JEWELRY

POTTER
CRAFT

NEW YORK

Copyright © 2007 by Nancy Alden

Photographs copyright © 2007 by William Brinson

Published in the United States by Potter Craft,
an imprint of the Crown Publishing Group,
a division of Random House, Inc., New York.
www.crownpublishing.com
www.pottercraft.com

POTTER CRAFT & Colophon and POTTER & Colophon are registered trademarks of Random House, Inc.

Library of Congress Cataloging-in-Publication Data is available by request.

ISBN 978-0-307-33952-2

Printed in China

Series Design by Lauren Monchik
Book Design by Amy Sly
Photography by William Brinson

1 3 5 7 9 8 6 4 2

First Edition

CONTENTS

INTRODUCTION

I have a long and close relationship with silver and gold. In fact, it was a problem with silver which set the pattern for much of my career. When I was seventeen, I apprenticed to a jeweler and set to work creating and selling silver jewelry.

Then, in the late seventies, a very strange thing happened: Two Texan brothers decided to try and corner the silver market. Over several months the cost of silver went up tenfold, until it was so expensive that people stopped buying silver jewelry. To stay in business, I turned to beads as the basic element of my designs. Immediately, a new world of materials was open to me and I was no longer at the mercy of the daily silver prices. But, although I departed from silver as a primary material, I understood well that both silver and gold would always retain a unique and permanent place in the creation of jewelry. They or their imitations are, quite simply, at the heart of almost all jewelry. Whether it is just a clasp, a line of spacer beads, or the central element of a design, one of these precious metals is nearly always a component of my work. So, while I am grateful that the greed of the Texan brothers forced me down a broader path, I am even more grateful that my early training gave me a deep understanding and respect for the twin foundations of jewelry design—silver and gold.

In this book I will try and give the reader the benefit of both these backgrounds as we explore how use these unique metals in the design and creation of fine beaded jewelry.

The most malleable of metals, silver and gold can be hammered or bent into whatever shape the designer needs. They are extremely ductile and can be stretched into fine wires or beaten into thin sheets, yet they have high tensile strength, which means they don't break easily.

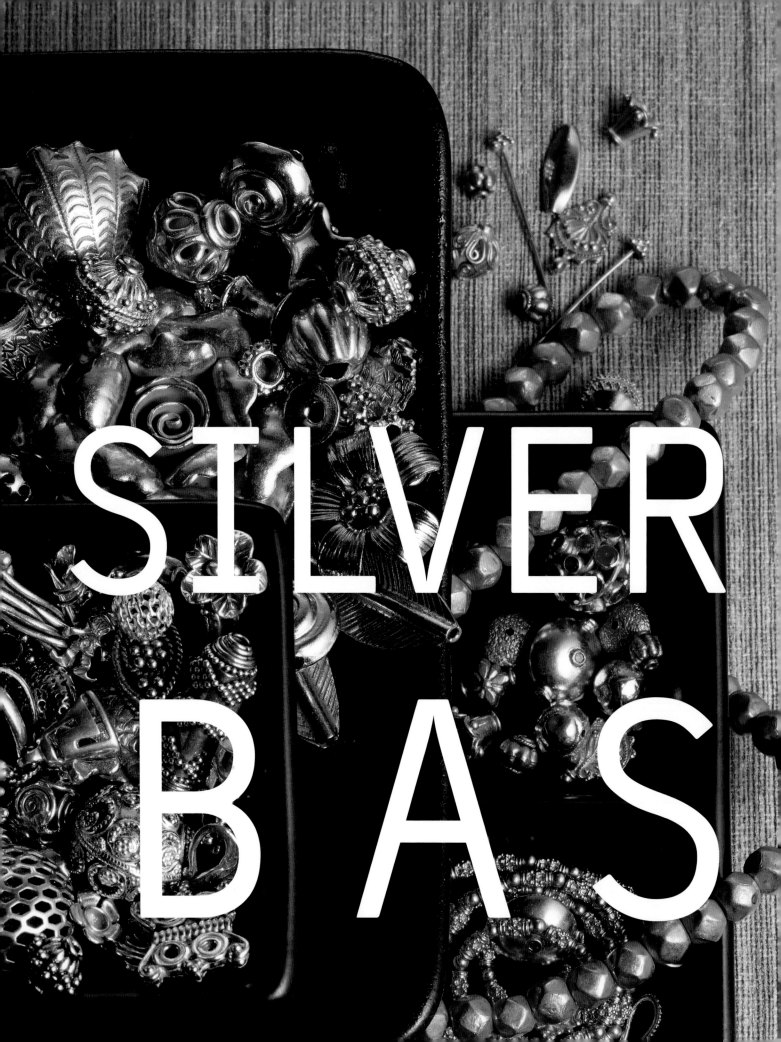

SILVER
BAS

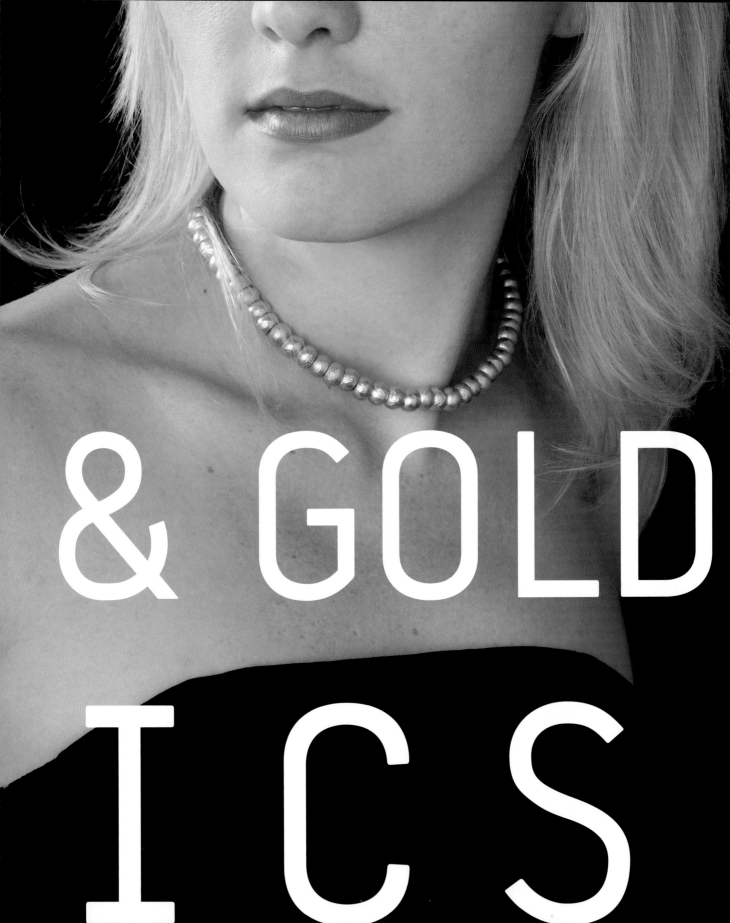

SILVER

Aside from its most visible presence as jewelry, silver has a truly surprising range of practical, sometimes essential, uses. For every ounce of silver used in jewelry or silverware, there are two ounces used for other purposes. Indeed, some of the characteristics that make silver so desirable for jewelry are those that also make it perfect for other jobs.

SUPPLY

Each year we dig up and refine less than a tenth of an ounce of silver for each person on the planet. This would work out to just one single decent size silver bead per person per year. It hardly seems enough!

But before you rush out to invest in this commodity in which demand so obviously outstrips supply, you must remember that a great deal of the silver dug up each year isn't consumed or destroyed—it is simply added to the constantly growing supply of above ground silver. Indeed, the silver you keep safely preserved in the form of jewelry, coins, and silverware helps to stabilize the price and provides a kind of emergency stockpile. Each year, new production of these items adds to the silver stocks of the previous centuries. Even industry manages to recycle most of its silver, thus conserving the supply.

New silver is dug from mines, but modern production has little in common with the romantic image of a glistening vein of solid silver offering itself to the miner's pickaxe. Silver is found in tiny quantities mixed with rock and other metals. Only by crushing huge amounts of these silver ores can one gather significant quantities of the precious metal. A ton of silver ore might yield only an ounce or two of pure silver. But only a third of silver even comes from a dedicated silver mine. Most of it is extracted from ores mined for other metals such as copper, lead, zinc, and gold.

VALUE

Silver has been the standard of moveable wealth for millennia. Along with gold, silver coins are the most ancient and persistent of currencies, in use since 8 BCE. To understand the importance of silver as money, consider the Maria Theresia Taler. This coin was first minted in 1741 during the reign of the Austrian Empress. In 1780, when its silver content was fixed at a constant twenty-eight grams, it became a highly valued international currency. Although Austria finally stopped

ALL THE SILVER IN THE WORLD
The traditional producers, Mexico and Peru have the highest output of silver, with the formidable mining resources of Australia coming close behind. Some sources are surprising: both Poland and China produce more silver than the United States or Canada. All in all, the world manages to produce or recycle more than 800 million ounces of silver each year.

regular production in 1996, more than 400 million were produced, and Maria Theresia Talers are still used as currency in parts of Africa and the Middle East. Although, with the exception of Mexico, all government mints have ceased to circulate coins containing real silver, they all understand the value of perception and use alloys that closely resemble the color of silver. And although not produced as circulating currency, every year more than 40 million ounces of silver are still turned into coins for investment.

Until the 1960s the price of silver was extremely stable, seldom falling below fifty cents an ounce or rising above a dollar fifty. This was because the American government effectively controlled its distribution and sat atop a hoard of some 2 billion ounces. As governments around the world stopped using real silver in their coinage or backing their currencies with precious metal, the U.S. Treasury began selling its stockpile, which was eagerly bought up by investors and industry. Price speculation spiraled out of control in the late 1970s when a pair of brothers from Texas famously tried to corner the market and silver briefly skyrocketed to fifty dollars an ounce. In recent years the commodity price of silver, controlled neither by governments nor by rampant speculation, has ranged between seven and fifteen dollars an ounce.

OTHER USES

Silver is the most reflective of all metals, outshining even gold. Once it is polished, it can reflect more than 95 percent of the light that hits its surface! For this reason, it not only sparkles on your finger or around your neck, but it is also the essential ingredient at the back of the finest mirrors. New technologies are sandwiching invisible silver coatings between glass panes to create windows that reflect the heat of the sun's rays or keep internal heat from escaping the room. And now it can be used to protect your eyes: silver halide crystals melted into the lenses of sunglasses keep out harmful rays of ultraviolet light.

Silver's resistance to corrosion and the "slippery" nature of its surface make it an attractive material for engineers. Next time you fly in a large aircraft, spare a moment of appreciation for the silver in its powerful engines. The rotating fans of a jet engine require faultless bearings so they can spin without creating too much friction. By regulation, they need to be able to do this even if, because of some mechanical failure, the essential lubricating fluids stop flowing. By plating the bearings with silver, engineers create bearings that will

FINDINGS KEY (PAGES 12–13, FROM LEFT TO RIGHT)

1. Hollow Thai Silver
2. Hollow Silver with Granulation
3. Silver Flat Squares with Grid Design
4. Silver Spacers
5. Silver Daisy Spacers
6. Vermeil Daisy Spacers
7. Hollow 18 Karat Gold with Resin Core
8. Perforated Silver Disc
9. Vermeil Spacer
10. Seamless Hollow Silver and Gold-Filled Round Spacers
11. Silver Wire Mesh
12. Silver Star Spacer
13. Silver Star Spacer
14. Silver Leaf
15. Vermeil Thai Leaf
16. Vermeil Thai Flower
17. Thai Silver Hollow Disc
18. Silver Spacer
19. Vermeil Disc
20. Vermeil
21. Perforated Hollow Vermeil
22. Silver Cylinder
23. Hollow Thai Silver "Shell"
24. Silver Double-Ended Bead Cap
25. Silver Cast To Imitate Granulation
26. Vermeil Thai Flower
27. Vermeil with Raised Silver
28. Silver Flat Square
29. Silver Barrel
30. Solid Silver Charm
31. Solid Silver Charm
32. Hollow 18 Karat Gold with Diamond
33. Solid Silver Charm
34. 18 Karat Gold Spacer
35. 18 Karat Gold Bead Cap
36. Silver "Birdcage"
37. Hollow Granulated Silver
38. Hollow Vermeil
39. 18 Karat Gold Pendant
40. 18 Karat Gold Filigree
41. Vermeil Star Spacer

1   2   3   4   5   6   7

not corrode and that have a high degree of lubricity, which enables them to keep the engine turning under extreme conditions.

Silver is a remarkably effective killer of bacteria. Ancient civilizations used silver vessels to keep water or wine pure. The expression "born with a silver spoon in his mouth" is attributed as much to health as to wealth. Feeding babies with a silver spoon was thought to ward off disease. Today, silver is used in modern water purification systems. Lacking the toxic qualities of lead (also a bacteria killer), silver compounds have become the preferred solder for the joints of household plumbing. Modern medicine also takes advantage of this characteristic of silver, and it is widely used in pharmaceutical and medical applications, such as ointments for burn victims.

Silver compounds are the preferred catalysts for many chemical reactions, and for some they are absolutely essential. The worldwide plastics industry relies on silver catalysts to create ethylene oxide, the building block for polyester textiles and a huge variety of molded plastic items. An amazing 700 tons of silver is in constant use worldwide just for this purpose.

Remarkably, the largest single use of silver is dedicated to creating the pictures in your photo album. Silver halide salts are at the heart of the photographic process. These salts react to light striking film to register an image. Although digital photography has stopped the growth of this use of silver, more than 150 million ounces a year are still consumed by the photographic industry.

GOLD

Although gold is no longer the most expensive metal on earth, it still reigns supreme as the most desired. Its historical worth and importance has never faltered—all cultures have attached a peculiar value to this delightful yellow metal. Yet, unlike silver, just a small portion of gold is used for practical applications.

SUPPLY

All the gold produced to date is estimated to be about 5 billion ounces. This figure is important because gold really is indestructible. Every piece of gold worn around the neck of some Greek princess or used to fashion the goblet of a wealthy Chinese merchant has been either preserved or recycled. Indeed, any gold jewelry you are wearing today most likely contains some gold that has been worn by others before. Still, more is always needed.

More than 90 percent of the total world supply of gold has been mined since the California gold rush of 1848. Due to new methods of extracting gold from the earth, the past few decades have added proportionately more than previous eras. More than 65 million ounces of gold are added each year, but the production process is no longer as simple as taking a pickaxe or a pan to recover visible pieces of gold. Mining today is a complex and expensive business. Great quantities of ore are blasted or dug from the earth to extract tiny amounts of gold—between three and ten parts per million parts of rock. Production costs can often exceed $400 an ounce. Yet, such is the market value of gold that producers literally go to the depths and heights of the world in search of it. The Savuka mine of South Africa operates at almost two miles below the surface, whereas Peru's Yanacocha mine, the second largest in the world, is located 14,000 feet above sea level.

VALUE

Throughout history gold has shared with silver the dominant role in all of the world's major currencies. Unlike silver, however, gold's monetary importance has persisted into the present day. Because gold is rare, easily shaped, and resistant to corrosion, its value for coinage was appreciated by the earliest civilizations. Since 6 BCE, gold coinage has been used throughout much of the world. It is so closely associated with money that it is considered indispensable, even in complex, industrial-era economies.

THE GOLDEN INDUSTRY OF JEWELRY
Almost two-thirds of the gold available in any one year goes to the production of jewelry or other decorative arts. Much of the rest simply gets locked away in vaults as private investments or central bank reserves.

In 1717 the great mathematician and head of the Royal Mint, Isaac Newton, fixed the price of a British gold guinea and launched three centuries of the Gold Standard as the mainstay of the world's monetary system. Right up until the 1970s, many of the world's major currencies were backed by a vast store of gold. In the case of the United States, its paper currency was supported by the promise that thirty-five dollars of it could be converted to an ounce of gold. Although the Gold Standard has since been abandoned and gold left to find its own value in the market place, major central banks still find it prudent to own large amounts of gold as a reserve.

While the Gold Standard was in force, the price of gold was fixed and there were many regulations to its trade. In 1975 the United States finally discarded the system, releasing people from the restrictions that had previously been placed on buying, selling, and owning gold. The price of gold, which had been held at an artificial rate for a hundred years, suddenly started climbing. Freed to find its place in the market, the price increased almost twenty-fold, finally peaking in 1980 at just greater than $800 an ounce. From there it settled back into a range of $300 to $400 an ounce. In the early years of the new millennium gold has recommenced its growth in value with a fairly steady climb up. Where it will go from here is anyone's guess, but for the moment, there are very few people betting against it.

OTHER USES

Like silver, gold is reflective, particularly of infrared light and harmful solar radiation. The cockpit windows of modern aircraft and the visors of space suits are both protected by a transparent sheet of gold film, and parts of lunar landing craft and other space vehicles are wrapped in gold-plated plastic to protect them from the sun's rays. Recordable compact discs also make use of the fact that gold will faithfully reflect a laser beam but does not tarnish like silver or copper.

Dentists have used gold for more than two thousand years because it has no harmful health effects and is resistant to corrosion. Today there are other alternatives, but gold alloys are still highly valued in crowns and fillings. Medicine also relies on the bio-compatibility of gold for other uses such as pacemaker wires and the plating of other implants. Compounds of gold have been found to be useful in the treatment of arthritis, and research is ongoing into their effect on other diseases.

CONTINENTS OF GOLD
Gold production is dominated by the continent of Africa, which produces about a quarter of the world's supply. North and South America each account for about a sixth. Australia, China, Russia, and Indonesia share much of the rest.

JEWELRY MAKING SUPPLIES

Before you rush out to buy any of the items listed below, carefully read the list of necessary ingredients and tools for the project you have in mind. Some require few tools or materials. In recent years, the proliferation of bead stores around the world has made it easy to acquire jewelry making supplies. If you do not have a local bead store, there are numerous mail-order suppliers, most of which offer online shopping.

TOOLS

It's surprising how few tools you need to make jewelry. For many necklaces and earrings, you can get away with just two: a pair of flat-nosed pliers and wire cutters. The other tools you need to make the designs in this book are detailed in "Toolbox Essentials."

Some of these items you can find around the house, but you'll want to make a modest investment in tools specifically designed for jewelry makers because they will make your life easier and your finished jewelry better.

There are other specialty items you can add as you go along, but the items in "Toolbox Essentials" are all you really need. Some people like to lay out their necklaces on a bead design board that has specially designed curved channels for holding beads. If you don't want to purchase one, you'll need to work with a bead mat or some other thick, soft material to keep your beads from rolling all over the place.

Like everything in life, beading tools come in levels of quality. Their cost depends on precision, sturdiness, and durability. If you are on a budget or think that your enthusiasm for making jewelry might be short-lived, you can buy cheap pliers to get yourself started. When you are hooked by the satisfaction and pleasure of creating your own jewelry, it will be time to upgrade—look for tools made in Germany. Once a passion for the craft sets in, you might want to splurge on a really superb set of Swedish cutters and pliers. But the important thing is just to get started.

TOOLBOX ESSENTIALS

- Wire cutters
- Narrow flat-nosed pliers
  (also known as chain-nosed pliers)
- Round-nosed pliers
- Awl (for designs on silk thread)
- Crimping pliers (only for designs that
  are strung on beading wire)
- Scissors
- Beading needle (twisted wire)
- Hypo-cement glue (or clear nail polish)

SPACERS

Spacers are just beads that create spaces between other larger or more important beads. Theoretically, all beads can act as spacers. In practice, however, spacers tend to be fairly simple silver and gold beads, although they are sometimes more elaborate. Their most important characteristic is that they should emphasize, rather than overwhelm, the main beads. Spacers do not always do this by being restricted in number: sometimes they are used sparsely, and sometimes they comprise the majority of the design. Nor are they necessarily restricted in beauty. A whole strand of gold daisy spacers, for instance, can be a thing of pleasure. The spacers' position in the design determines their character. Spacers are beads that know when to hold back and let others take the central role.

STRINGING MATERIAL

The main structure of a neck "lace" is, by definition, a piece of thin material that can be wrapped like a lace around the neck. This material can be silk thread, leather thong, wire, chain, or one of the modern bead-stringing wires. Whatever the material, it must combine both strength and flexibility. Here are the stringing materials we recommend in *Simply Silver, Simply Gold:*

SILK

This traditional material is still preferred for threading beads and designs where the thread is to be knotted between the beads. It is reasonably strong, easy to work with and very, very supple. While modern beading wire is stronger and easier to use, no other material allows a strand of beads to embrace the neck in quite the same way as silk. But silk has some distinct disadvantages: it will break when roughly handled, it will stretch over time, and it gets dirty. Because of this, any beads strung on silk will have to be re-strung periodically. How frequently depends on how much you are wearing them. But a good rule of thumb is that necklaces that are worn regularly should be re-strung every one or two years.

Silk comes in several thicknesses which are expressed by an arcane alphabetical code. The thickest silk thread is FFF, while the thinnest is size 00. For all our projects, we are going to use size F and keep things simple.

BEADING WIRE

Modern technology has tried to overcome the disadvantages of silk, while retaining its qualities of flexibility and ease of use. This was a suprisingly difficult task and the only material to come close is a relatively new and sophisticated product. Beading wire seems simple: it's just a few twisted strands of wire coated in plastic. But early attempts were frustratingly inadequate. The wire was too stiff to lie around the neck gracefully; it would kink if bent sharply and it would break if mishandled. The problems were solved by twisting more and more strands of thinner wire to add both flexibility and strength. Today's 19 and 49-strand beading wires are increasingly kink-resistant; they don't break under normal use and, although still not quite as supple as silk, they are very flexible. With the logic of an industry more used to hardware than jewelry, the manufacturers of beading wire have decided to measure its thickness in inches. This completely ignores the fact that the holes in beads are measured in millimeters. Wherever "beading wire" is called for in the materials list we recommend using the best quality 49-strand size .015. If a thinner or thicked wire is called for, it is specified in the list.

CHAIN

Whatever style of chain you prefer, I recommend that you use only sterling silver and gold-filled. Plated chain is cheaper, but deteriorates quickly and is not an appropriate material to use with gemstones. Solid gold chain is, of course, nice to have, but very expensive. In appearance and durability, gold-filled chain is the next best thing.

WIRE

Stringing beads together with wire is easier than it first appears. In these designs we use just two types: sterling silver and gold-filled, both in a "half-hard" density. Wire is sold in another traditional measurement, "gauge". The wires used in these designs are either 20 or 22 gauge, corresponding to .032 and .025 of an inch.

ELASTIC THREAD

A wonderfully simple material to use for bracelets. Since it can be knotted, no tools or findings are needed. Although they are not as durable as beading wire and should not be used for very expensive beads, modern beading elastics are suprisingly strong and long lasting under normal wear.

SILK TIP

AFTER THREADING YOUR NEEDLE, RUN THE SILK ACROSS A BLOCK OF BEESWAX. THIS WILL KEEP THE THREAD TOGETHER AND HELP PREVENT FRAYING.

FINDINGS FOR NECKLACES

These linking pieces are the jewelry maker's essential hardware. Just as the carpenter fills his toolbox with the nails, screws, and bolts needed to construct his works, so the jeweler has her stock of clasps, wires, and links. There are many hundreds of different findings, but you need know only a few to make the jewelry in *Simply Silver, Simply Gold*. Most findings come in different metals, and you should always use the one that is appropriate to the design. The basic materials are listed on page 21.

BEAD TIPS

Bead tips attach the end of a necklace thread to the clasp. The tip is designed to grip onto the knot you make after stringing the last bead, and it comes in two varieties, the basket bead tip and the clamshell. The former works by trapping the knot in a little basket, while the latter sandwiches the knot between two concave wings that look like clamshells.

CRIMPS

Crimps are tiny metal beads that can be crushed flat with pliers. Beading wire is first threaded through the bead crimp, then through the loop of a clasp, and then back through the crimp. Finally, the little crimp is firmly but carefully squashed to attach the wire to the clasp. There is even a specialty tool, crimping pliers, that helps exert the right amount of pressure to make a perfect seal. You can also close crimps with simple flat-nosed pliers.

CLASPS

Clasps for necklaces and bracelets come in a staggering variety. Several different methods are used to attach the two halves of a clasp, but all the styles are attached to the necklace pretty much the same way.

CRIMP COVERS

These provide an easy way of disguising the messy part of the necklace between the clasp and the first and last beads. They are hollow spheres which open up like clamshells. You simply fit them over the flattened crimp and squeeze them gently shut. Once in place, they look just like a smooth round silver or gold bead. Although these findings are not necessary for the construction of a necklace, they can add an extra touch of sophistication to your designs.

STYLES OF CLASPS
- Hook and eye
- Fish hook
- Box
- Toggle
- Lobster claw
- Spring ring
- Sliding

FINDINGS FOR EARRINGS AND NECKLACES

EARWIRES

Earrings for pierced ears use earwires designed to fit through the pierced hole. Other earrings use earwires that clamp on to the earlobe with a clip or a screw. Earwires for pierced ears should always be of good quality and made from material that does not cause an allergic reaction.

HEADPINS AND EYEPINS

These are simple pieces of straight wire on which you thread your beads. The "head" or "eye" at one end keeps the beads from falling off, and the other end is attached to the beading wire, chain, or earwire.

JUMP RINGS, SPLIT RINGS, AND PLAIN RINGS

These findings are often used for linking parts of necklaces and earrings. A jump ring is a simple metal loop that can be opened and closed by twisting. A split ring cannot be opened, but the item to be connected can be slipped onto it by feeding the item around the split in the side of the ring. (Split rings are just miniature versions of the metal rings on key chains.) A plain ring is one that cannot be opened because the ends are soldered together.

FINDINGS MATERIALS

GOLD
Use only with gems of high value.

GOLD-FILLED
Use with any good gems.

VERMEIL (sterling silver plated with gold)
Use with modest value gems or good quality glass.

NIOBIUM (hypo-allergenic metal)
Use if you have an allergic reaction to silver.

SILVER (sterling or better)
Use with gems or good quality glass and other good quality materials.

PLATED BASE METAL
Use only with the very cheapest materials.

FINDINGS KEY (PAGES 22–23, FROM LEFT TO RIGHT)

PAGE 22

1. Gold-Filled Shepherd's Hook Earwire (Left) "Add-On" Earwire (Right)
2. Silver and Gold-Filled Crimp Beads
3. Silver Bead Caps
4. Silver Leverback Earwire (Left) Earwire with Ball (Right)
5. Silver Bead Caps
6. Silver and Gold-Filled Crimp Covers
7. Antiqued Silver Bead Caps
8. Silver And Gold-Filled Basket Bead Tips
9. Vermeil Headpins With Ball Tip
10. Gold-Filled Headpins
11. Silver and Gold-Filled Eyepin
12. Silver and Gold-Filled Rings
13. Silver Jump Rings
14. Silver and Vermeil Headpins With Ball Tip

PAGE 23

15. Gold-Filled Lobster Clasp
16. Silver And Marcasite Toggle Clasp
17. Vermeil Lobster Clasp
18. Silver Box Clasp
19. Silver and Marcasite Toggle Clasp
20. Gold-Filled Box Clasp
21. Gold-Filled Box Clasp
22. Gold-Filled Lobster Clasp
23. Vermeil Toggle Clasp
24. "Stardust" Silver Toggle Clasp
25. Vermeil Lobster Clasp
26. Silver Hook and Eye Clasp
27. Silver Toggle Clasp
28. Vermeil Toggle Clasp
29. Silver Hook and Eye Clasp
30. Gold-Filled Three-Strand Sliding Clasp
31. Silver Hook and Eye Clasp
32. Gold-Filled Spring Ring Clasp
33. Silver Toggle Clasp

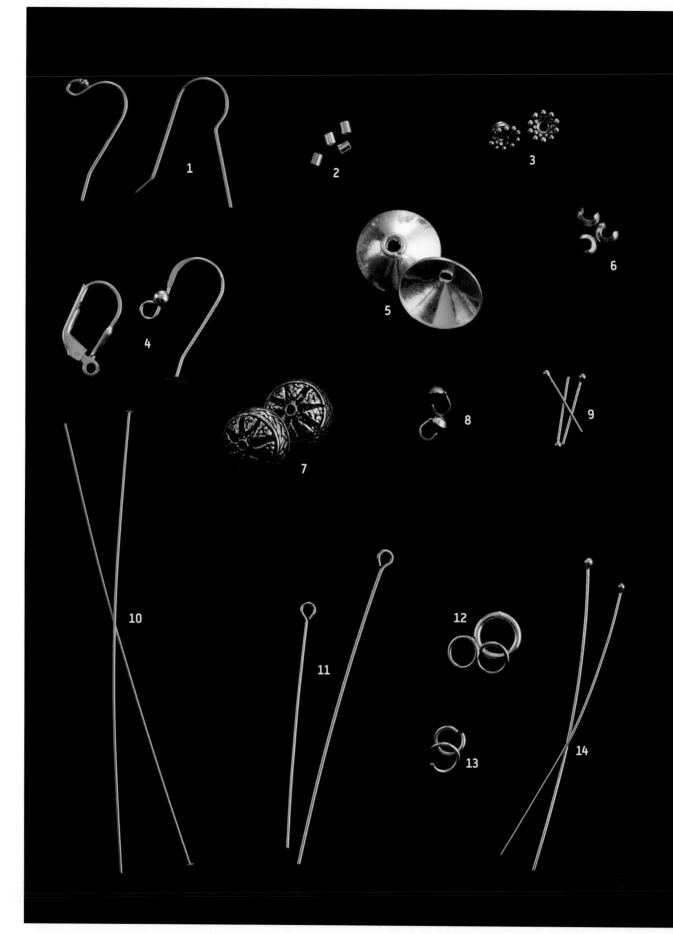

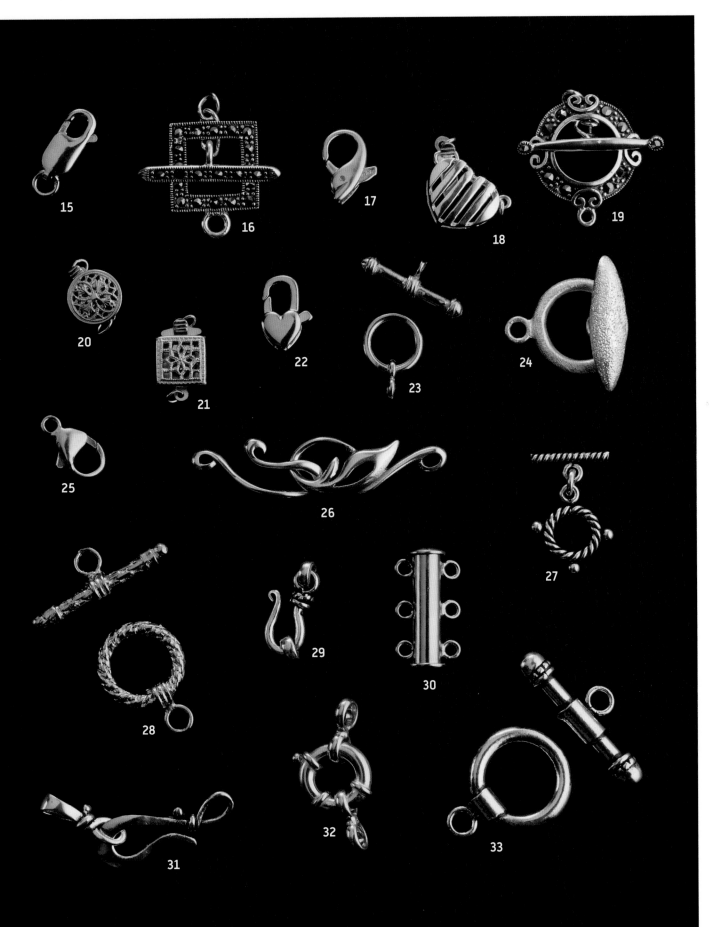

15

16

17

18

19

20

21

22

23

24

25

26

27

28

29

30

31

32

33

THE QUALITIES OF SILVER AND GOLD

WHAT DO WE MEAN BY SILVER?

Although one of silver's greatest attributes is malleability, it is, in truth, just a little too soft to be ideal for making durable objects. To increase its hardness, it is customary to add a little of another metal, usually copper. Because this practice is both ancient and widespread, a universal standard has developed: to be considered silver, an item must contain at least 92.5 percent silver. This is the definition of sterling silver, a term that was already in use in twelfth-century England.

It is common to stamp larger silver objects with either the word *silver* or the number 925, which describes the fineness of the silver. Sterling silver has a fineness of 925 because it is 925 parts silver and 75 parts copper or other metal. In this book, when we say silver, we mean sterling.

THE COLOR OF GOLD

Fine or pure gold has a constant color, which is a slightly orange shade of yellow. When gold is alloyed with other metals, however, the color changes—sometimes dramatically. Some colors have come to be closely related to the karat value of the gold, while others have taken on a distinctive name like white, rose, or green gold. To preserve a color close to fine gold, producers use a balance of copper and silver. If they add more copper, the gold becomes redder; more silver, and it gets whiter. A little zinc or other metal is sometimes added to vary other characteristics of the alloy. White gold employs the bleaching qualities of palladium or nickel to achieve its silvery appearance, although it is often enhanced by a plating of rhodium. For most of us, the essential pleasing color of gold is yellow with just a touch of red.

KARATS AND CARATS

There are so many confusing measurements in the jewelry industry, but surely the most confusing expressions are karat and carat. The word (for they really are the same word despite the difference of an initial letter) is derived from the ancient Greek *keration*, or carob bean. As such, it was a unit of small weight, which became popular for measuring precious stones and metals. Because beans tend to vary in weight from place to place, there was a degree of variation and

OTHER TYPES OF SILVER

In northern Thailand, silversmiths use a softer silver to make it easier to form their intricate beads. The fineness of Thai silver can be anywhere from 950 to 985. Mexican jewelry also uses a 950 silver, which is softer than sterling. The expression *fine silver* refers to the highest grades of .999 and greater.

uncertainty for many centuries. In 1913, the United States settled on a metric carat, or 200 milligrams, as the measurement for the weight of gemstones, and this has since become the global standard.

KARAT GOLDS

Pure gold is also considered too soft for most jewelry: Gold alloys are a compromise of strength, hardness, color, and value. Throughout the world, 18 karat gold has a fineness of 750 and always contains 75 percent gold and 25 percent something else. The most popular karat golds are listed below with their percentages of pure gold and the corresponding fineness.

GOLD ALLOY STANDARDS

KARATS	% GOLD (FINENESS)	COMMENT
24	99% (990)	Popular in China and some other parts of the Far East
22	91.6% (916)	Popular standard in India
18	75% (750)	Most common global standard for gold jewelry
14	58.5% (585)	Popular standard in North America
12	50% (500)	Minimum to be described as gold in much of the world
10	41.7% (417)	Minimum to be described as gold in United States
9	37.5% (375)	Minimum to be described as gold in Canada and the U.K.

Many European countries insist that any items sold as gold are hallmarked or stamped by a government assayer's office to indicate their fineness. In North America, gold jewelry must be described by its karat quality, but independent assaying and physical marking is not required by law. Small items, such as individual beads, that would be ruined by stamping should be accompanied by an invoice or document marked with the karat quality and the name of the company that stands behind the mark.

Although to the layman a "heart of solid gold" seems straightforward, a jeweler would need to know whether that heart was 18 karat or mere 10 karat, for solid gold does not refer to its purity, only to the fact that the item is not hollow. The proportion of actual gold in a piece of jewelry is only determined by the karat mark or statement of fineness.

"PURE" GOLD

Although gold must be at least 99 percent pure to be 24 karat, there is also 24 karat fine gold which is 99.9 percent pure and used mainly for investment quality coins and bullion.

JUST SILVER

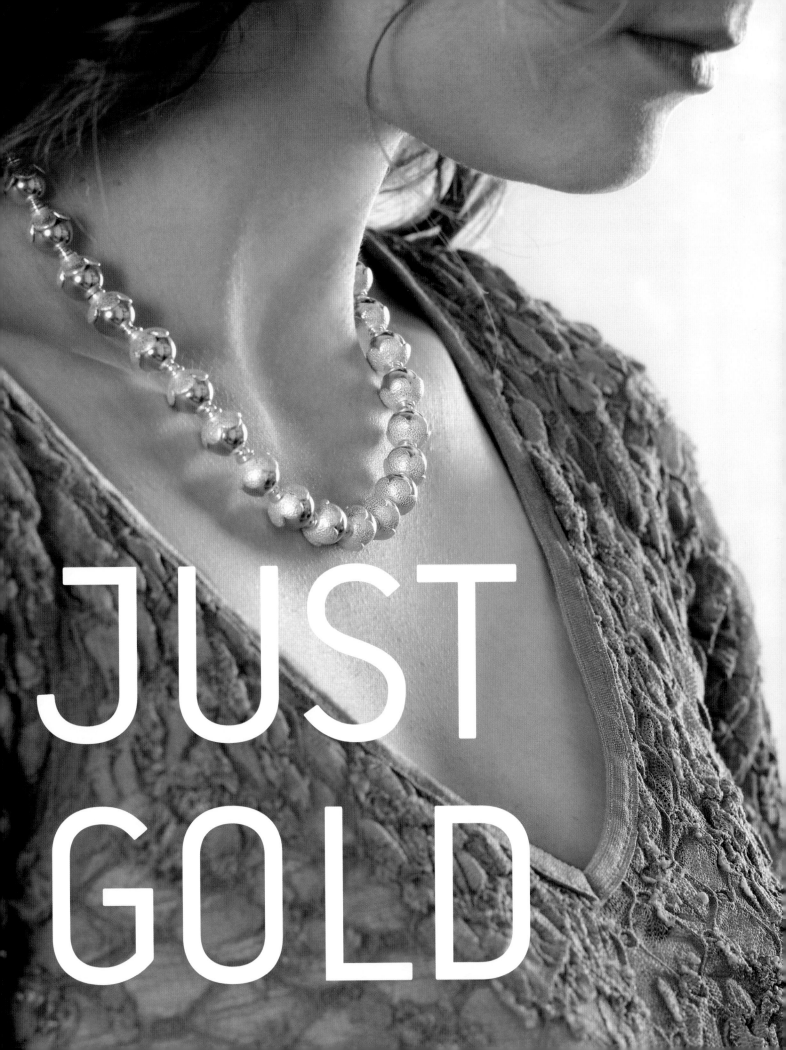

JUST
GOLD

MAKING JEWELRY WITH SILVER AND GOLD

Making necklaces and earrings is simplicity itself. Although you still have to turn to a professional jeweler for setting rings and casting metals, you can master the basic techniques of stringing beads and bending wire in an evening. Combine these simple skills with a few inexpensive tools, add the basic ingredients of beads and findings, and you are ready to start making your own jewelry. Don't be intimidated! Compared to preparing a decent meal, making a piece of jewelry is child's play—it not only takes fewer tools, but also leaves no dishes to wash up!

Every necklace or pair of earrings begins with a design. While it is perfectly possible to throw random beads on a string, it's very unlikely that the results will be satisfying. My approach to jewelry design begins with a simple premise: "The purpose of any body decoration is to enhance the look of the wearer." I care, therefore, that the design will go well with the wearer's face as well as with her clothes, her mood, and the impression she wishes to make. Some designers might disagree and view the body as a convenient frame for exhibiting an interesting object. If you are making jewelry for yourself, however, you will probably be more sympathetic to the view that the jewels are there to make you look good—not the other way around.

While the jewelry designs in this book are in every way contemporary, they are integrated with classic styles and materials that consistently return to the forefront of fashion and have a proven record of making their owners feel they are wearing the "right stuff."

Although you can follow the project instructions and replicate the jewelry in this book as shown in the photographs, do not be reluctant to experiment and add your own touches. You should think of the instructions as recipes in which even small changes of ingredients can create a different but delightful flavor. As in cooking, you should not be afraid to substitute and create your own unique "dish." Making these designs will, after all, be even more rewarding if they include a dash of your own creative style.

It is my hope that, after you have made a few of the projects in this book, you will use your skills and your own design sense to introduce variations and start creating entirely new designs of your own.

HOW TO CREATE YOUR OWN DESIGNS

Whether substituting ingredients or planning a whole new design, you should follow these basic guidelines:

1. Do not mix inappropriate materials. While it is obvious that you would not use real gold with plated plastic, other combinations are less obvious no-nos. In case you are not yet ready to trust your own eye, chapter 3, "Designing with Other Beads," includes suggestions for gems and other materials that mix beautifully with silver and gold.

2. Never use materials that look cheap, no matter what they actually cost. They will make the good look bad.

3. Use materials that will be in fashion for decades rather than for weeks. Today's fad is toast tomorrow.

Before you attempt any of the projects in this book, you will need to read the instructions for basic jewelry making in chapter 4, "Jewelry Techniques." This chapter contains information on stringing, making continuous strands, attaching clasps, wrapping wire, measuring, and using essential tools. Read chapter 4 carefully, but note that these techniques are best learned through actual practice. When you feel comfortable, jump in and get started. As with all crafts, the only way to master the art of jewelry making is by actually doing it.

DESIGNING FOR YOU

When you are making jewelry for yourself or for friends and family, you have the opportunity to create something that is truly customized. Try matching the colors with favorite clothes, skin and hair tones, or other preferences. Also consider size. Bigger necks and busts obviously call for longer necklaces, but the actual bead size can be just as important. In designing commissioned pieces, I always first consider the shape of the client—the more delicate her bone structure, the more delicate the jewelry.

While fashion and mood will dictate overall bead sizes, the general rule "bigger women need bigger beads" is a good one to follow. There are always exceptions, but size in jewelry is as important as size in clothing. No piece should overwhelm, or be overwhelmed by, the body it adorns. In jewelry design, the goal is harmony, not competition.

1.
SOLID SILVER BRACELET

THIS IS A GREAT WAY TO USE LOVELY AND UNUSUALLY SHAPED BEADS. THE BEADS ARE LIKE LITTLE COFFEE BEANS WITH A PATTERN ON EACH END. FIT THEM SNUGLY IN PAIRS AND THEY CREATE A SOLID ROPE AROUND THE WRIST FULL OF TEXTURE AND REFLECTION. BECAUSE THE BEADS ARE SOLID SILVER AND TIGHTLY PACKED TOGETHER, THE DESIGN IS A BIT TOO HEAVY FOR A NECKLACE, BUT IT LOOKS AND FEELS WONDERFUL AS A BRACELET FOR OCCASIONS THAT DEMAND A POWERFUL STATEMENT.

1. Start the bracelet by threading on a crimp. Pass the beading wire through the ring of one half of the clasp back through the crimp. Make sure that the beading wire is tight around the ring and squeeze the crimp shut. Add a crimp cover.

2. Thread on a bean bead so that the concave, or inside, of the bean curves around the crimp cover and hides the tail of the beading wire. Add another bean so that its back is against the back of the first. Now add another so that the concave side fits snugly into the concave side of the second bean bead. Repeat this pattern of pairs of bean beads seventeen times or until the bracelet is the length you wish.

3. Add a final 2.5mm round bead and a crimp. Bring the beading wire through the ring of the other side of the clasp and back through the crimp and round bead. Tighten the bracelet so there are no spaces between the beads, then close the crimp and snip off any remaining beading wire. Add the remaining crimp cover.

4. To make the dangle, use the headpin and add a round bead, a pair of bean beads, and another round bead. Use your round-nosed pliers to grip the headpin about $1/4$" above the bead. Make a loop, attach it to the ring of the clasp, and wrap the tail of the headpin between the bottom of the loop and the top of the bead. (See "Wire-Wrapping" in Jewelry Techniques, page 129.)

TOOLS
Wire Cutters, Crimping Pliers, Round-Nosed Pliers

MATERIALS

2	silver crimp beads
10"	of beading wire
1	silver toggle clasp
2	silver crimp covers
39	5mm by 10mm solid silver "bean"-shaped beads
3	2.5mm hollow silver seamless round beads
1	1" silver headpin with ball tip

NOTE
Attaching a dangle to the clasp of a bracelet is not just a decorative feature. The weight of the dangle helps to ensure that the clasp of the bracelet will fall on the underside of your wrist.

2.
HOLLOW SILVER BRACELET

VARY THIS WITH GEMSTONES, SILVER OR GOLD ROUND BEADS.

1. Start by threading on a crimp. Pass the wire through the ring of half of the clasp back through the crimp. Tighten the beading wire around the ring and squeeze the crimp shut.

2. Thread on a black onyx followed by a disc bead. Repeat this pattern 11 times or until the bracelet fits. (Try it around your wrist.)

3. Bring the beading wire through the ring of the other side of the clasp and back through the crimp and round bead. Now tighten the bracelet so there are no spaces between the beads, close the crimp and snip off any remaining beading wire.

TOOLS
Wire Cutters, Crimping Pliers

MATERIALS
- 12   11 by 5mm hollow silver disc shape beads
- 13   3mm black onyx round beads
- 1   silver pendulum clasp
- 24   silver crimp beads
- 2   crimp bead covers
- 10"   of beading wire

3.
SPACER NECKLACE

THE BEADS IN THIS DESIGN WOULD BE USED AS SPACERS IN OTHER NECKLACES. HERE THEY BALANCE EACH OTHER TO CREATE AN EQUAL PARTNERSHIP.

1. Start the necklace by threading on a crimp. Pass the beading wire through the ring of one half of the clasp back through the crimp. Make sure that the beading wire is tight around the ring and squeeze the crimp shut. Add a silver spacer bead to cover the tail of the beading wire and cut.

2. Thread on a round bead and a spacer bead. Repeat pattern 63 times.

3. Add the remaining crimp and bring the wire through the ring of the other side of the clasp and back through the crimp and last spacer. Tighten so that all the beads fit snugly. Close the crimp and snip off any remaining wire. Add the crimp covers.

TOOLS
Wire Cutters, Crimping Pliers

MATERIALS
- 2   silver crimp beads
- 20"   of beading wire
- 1   silver ring clasp
- 64   3mm granulated silver spacer beads
- 63   4mm seamless hollow silver round beads
- 2   silver crimp covers

4.
SILVER TREASURE NECKLACE

SOME SILVER BEADS ARE SO ELABORATE THAT THEY ARE LIKE LITTLE TREASURES. I LOVE TO TAKE AN ASSORTMENT OF MY MOST TREASURED SILVER BEADS AND PUT THEM TOGETHER SO THAT NO SINGLE ONE IS REPEATED. SOME OF THESE BEADS ARE GRANULATED, OTHERS ARE FORMED WITH SILVER WIRE AND SHEETS. THEY ARE ALL BEAUTIFUL, AND EACH COULD STAND ALONE AS A CENTERPIECE OR HIGHLIGHT. DO NOT TRY TO COPY THE BEADS EXACTLY, BUT GATHER TOGETHER AN ASSORTMENT OF YOUR OWN FAVORITE BEADS.

1. Start by attaching each of the treasure beads to a piece of looped wire in the following manner: Use your round-nosed pliers to make a simple loop at the end of the silver wire (see "Using Headpins" in Jewelry Techniques, page 128). Choose a round silver bead that is big enough that it will not go through the hole in the treasure bead and that is appropriate to the overall size of the treasure bead. Thread it on to the wire, then add the treasure bead and another round bead. Make sure they are snug against each other and the loop, then cut the wire about 1/4" above the last bead. Make a simple loop ensuring that the bottom of the loop fits snugly against the round bead. Repeat this process for the rest of the treasure beads.

2. Arrange the treasure beads in a pleasing order so that there is a balance between the larger and smaller beads. Slightly open the ring on one end of the toggle clasp, slip on a twisted wire ring, and close. Slightly open the loop at one end of the first treasure bead. Attach it to the twisted wire ring and close. Open the loop at the other end of the treasure bead and attach another twisted wire ring. Use this to attach the next treasure bead. Repeat this process until all the beads are used or until the necklace is the length you want. Attach the other half of the clasp.

3. To make the dangles, add a spacer bead or a round silver bead or a combination of both to a 1/2" headpin. Make a simple loop. Attach these dangles to ten of the links of the necklace, spacing them in a pleasing manner.

TOOLS
Round-Nosed Pliers, Wire Cutters, Crimping Pliers

MATERIALS (TO MAKE A 30" ROPE LENGTH)

5"	(approximately) of 20-gauge silver wire
74	assorted 2.5mm and 4mm seamless hollow silver beads
29	assorted silver beads ranging from 9mm to 20mm in width
1	silver toggle clasp
30	5mm silver twisted wire rings
6	5mm "Balinese"-style spacer beads
10	1/2" silver headpins with ball tip

5.
GRANULATED SILVER NECKLACE

THESE BEAUTIFUL BEADS ARE MADE USING THE TIME-CONSUMING GRANULATION METHOD. STARTING WITH A HOLLOW SILVER BALL, THE ARTISAN ADDS HUNDREDS OF TINY GRANULES OF SILVER TO MAKE THE PATTERN ON EACH BEAD. THIS STYLE IS SOMETIMES CALLED BALINESE, BUT IT IS ALSO USED IN INDIA AND OTHER PARTS OF THE WORLD.

1. Start the necklace by threading on a crimp. Pass the beading wire through the ring of one half of the clasp and back through the crimp. Make sure that the beading wire is tight around the ring and squeeze the crimp shut.

2. Thread on one black onyx bead and one silver bead. Repeat this pattern twenty times.

3. Add a another black onyx bead and a crimp. Bring the beading wire through the ring of the other side of the clasp and back through the crimp and round bead. Tighten the necklace so there are no spaces between the beads, then close the crimp and snip off any remaining beading wire. Add the crimp covers.

TOOLS
Wire Cutters, Crimping Pliers

MATERIALS
- 2 silver crimp beads
- 20" of beading wire
- 1 silver toggle clasp
- 22 3mm black onyx round beads
- 21 15mm "Balinese"-style hollow silver beads
- 2 silver crimp bead covers

6.
GRANULATED SILVER EARRINGS

THIS IS AN INCREDIBLY SIMPLE WAY TO MAKE A PAIR OF EARRINGS TO ACCOMPANY THE GRANULATED SILVER NECKLACE (SEE PAGE 35). IT USES A SPECIAL EARWIRE SHAPED LIKE A "V" WITH A BALL ON ONE OF THE TIPS.

1. Slip a bead onto the side of the earwire without the ball tip. Very slowly and gently bend the apex of the "V" until you can just get the bead around to the other side.

TOOLS
None

MATERIALS
- 2 15mm "Balinese"-style hollow silver beads
- 2 2" V-shaped silver earwires with a thin side of 1mm and the thicker side about 1.5mm

7.
HOLLOW GOLD

ALTHOUGH THESE LOVELY HAND-CAST GOLD BEADS ARE COMPLETELY HOLLOW AND VERY LIGHT, THEIR UNEVEN EXTERIOR GIVES AN IMPRESSION OF SOLIDITY. BY MIMICKING THE ROUGH SURFACE OF GOLD NUGGETS, THEY LOOK AS IF THEY WERE SOLID GOLD.

1. Start the necklace by threading on a crimp. Pass the beading wire through the ring of one half of the clasp back through the crimp. Make sure that the beading wire is tight around the ring and squeeze the crimp shut.

2. Now thread on the 60 gold beads. Try the necklace around your neck for size and add or subtract beads as necessary.

3. Bring the beading wire through the ring of the other side of the clasp and back through the crimp and round bead. Now tighten the necklace so that all the beads fit snugly. Close the crimp and snip off any remaining beading wire. Add the crimp covers.

USING HOLLOW SILVER OR GOLD BEADS GREATLY REDUCES THE COST, AS WELL AS THE WEIGHT, OF YOUR JEWELRY. FOR THIS REASON ALONE, THEY ARE POPULAR AND USEFUL BEADS. THEIR LIGHT WEIGHT ALSO APPEALS TO MANY PEOPLE BECAUSE THEY FIND THE JEWELRY MORE COMFORTABLE TO WEAR. BUT LET'S NOT RATIONALIZE ECONOMY TOO MUCH—THERE ARE TIMES WHEN A GIRL JUST WANTS TO FEEL ALL THAT PRECIOUS METAL AS WELL AS SEE IT! HEAVY CHUNKS OF SILVER OR GOLD ARE PLEASANT REMINDERS THAT ONE IS WEARING SOMETHING OF REAL VALUE.

TOOLS
Wire Cutters, Crimping Pliers

MATERIALS

2	gold-filled crimp beads
20"	of beading wire
1	18 karat gold toggle clasp
60	6mm by 9mm 18 karat gold hollow rondel beads
2	gold-filled crimp covers

8.
SIMPLY GOLD

IN THIS ALL-GOLD NECKLACE, THE LITTLE HOLLOW ROUND BEADS
SEEM JUST AS SOLID AND SUBSTANTIAL AS THE GRANULATED
BEADS, WHICH GIVES THE PIECE THE FEELING OF REAL GOLD.
THE CENTRAL PENDANT CHARM PRESENTS AN EXTRAVAGANT
GOLD FACE BUT ECONOMIZES BY BEING VERY THIN.

1. Start the necklace by threading on a crimp. Pass the beading
   wire through the ring of one half of the clasp back through the
   crimp. Make sure that the beading wire is tight around the ring
   and squeeze the crimp shut. Add 3 gold round beads to cover
   the tail of the beading wire and cut.

2. Now thread on a granulated bead, followed by a round bead.
   Repeat this pattern another twenty-eight times. Add the 18 karat
   gold charm and repeat the same pattern twenty-nine times on
   the other side. Try the necklace around your neck for size and
   add or subtract beads as necessary.

3. Add the final two round beads and the crimp bead and bring the
   beading wire through the ring of the other side of the clasp and
   back through the crimp and round beads. Now tighten the necklace so that all the beads fit snugly. Close the crimp and snip off
   any remaining beading wire. Add the crimp covers.

TOOLS
Wire Cutters, Crimping Pliers

MATERIALS

2	gold-filled crimp beads
20"	of beading wire
1	18 karat gold hook-and-eye clasp
64	2mm 18 karat gold seamless hollow round beads
58	4mm by 2mm 18 karat gold "Balinese"-style granulated beads
1	18 karat gold charm
2	gold-filled crimp covers

LAZY DAISY BRACELET | SILVER AND GOLD

9.
SILVER AND GOLD

THE SLIGHTLY DIFFERENT SHAPES OF THE GOLD AND THE SILVER
BEADS CONTRAST WITHOUT BREAKING UP THE IMPRESSION OF A
SOLID BAND OF PRECIOUS METAL.

1. Start the necklace by creating the beaded loop which will hold
   the large "double lobster" clasp. Thread on a crimp bead then
   eight 3mm gold-filled round beads. Pass the beading wire
   through the clasp ring and back through the crimp. Make sure
   that the loop of beads is tight and sits nicely around the clasp,
   then squeeze the crimp shut. Add a 7mm silver round bead to
   cover the crimp and the tail of the beading wire and cut.

2. Thread on a gold-filled rondel and a 7mm silver round bead.
   Repeat 38 times or until the necklace is the length you wish.

3. Add a final 7mm silver bead and a 3mm gold filled bead.

4. Add the remaining crimp bead and bring the beading wire
   through the ring and back through the crimp and the last gold-
   filled and silver round beads. Now tighten the necklace so that
   all the beads fit snugly against each other. Close the crimp and
   snip off any remaining beading wire. Add the crimp cover.

TOOLS
Wire Cutters, Crimping Pliers

MATERIALS

39	gold-filled seamless hollow rondel beads
40	7mm silver seamless hollow round beads with large holes
9	3mm gold-filled seamless hollow round beads
2	silver or gold-filled crimp bead
1	silver crimp cover
1	6mm gold-filled ring
1	silver "double lobster" clasp
	20" of beading wire

NOTE
Although elastic is not a particularly strong
or durable material, it is wonderfully
tempting to use for bracelets. This design
takes mere moments to make, yet delivers
an elegant and rich looking adornment.

10.
LAZY DAISY BRACELET

1. Attach a piece of tape to one end of the elastic so that the
   beads do not fall off. Then string on one gold-filled bead and
   nine silver daisy beads. Repeat this pattern eight times.

2. Take the two loose ends of the elastic cord and make an overhand knot. Tighten it so that all the beads are firmly together.
   There should not be any spaces between the beads, but do not
   over tighten. Make a second overhand knot on top of the first,
   being careful not to allow the cord to slacken and create any
   gaps. Apply a drop of clear nail polish to the knot. Once the
   knot is dry, tuck it inside the hole of the gold bead to hide it.

TOOLS
Clear Nail Polish

Scotch tape

MATERIALS

10"	of .08 clear elastic beading cord
9	7mm gold-filled seamless hollow round beads
81	4mm silver daisy spacer beads

11.
GOLD WITH SILVER CAPS

USING A BEAD CAP CAN SOMETIMES PRODUCE AN EXCITING NEW LOOK FOR AN ORDINARY BEAD. HERE, THE SILVER CAP FITS SO TIGHTLY AROUND THE PLAIN ROUND GOLD BEAD THAT IT SEEMS AS IF THE SILVER HAS BEEN FUSED TO THE GOLD, FORMING A SINGLE INTRICATE DESIGN.

1. Start the necklace by threading on a crimp. Pass the beading wire through the ring of one half of the clasp back through the crimp. Make sure that the beading wire is tight around the ring and squeeze the crimp shut. Add a gold round bead cover the tail of the beading wire and cut.

2 Now thread on a silver 2.5mm bead and a gold 2.5mm bead, then the gold 4mm bead.

3. Add a silver bead cap, a 9mm gold bead and a 3mm silver bead. Repeat this pattern 33 times but for the last silver round bead use a 4mm bead instead of 3mm. Try the necklace around your neck to make sure it is the correct length.

4. Add the final gold and silver 2.5mm beads. Bring the beading wire through the ring of the other side of the clasp and back through the crimp and round beads. Now tighten the necklace so that all the bead caps fit snugly on the round beads. Close the crimp and snip off any remaining beading wire. Add the final crimp cover.

TOOLS
Wire Cutters, Crimping Pliers

MATERIALS

34	9mm seamless hollow gold-filled round beads
34	10mm silver bead caps
2	2.5mm seamless hollow silver beads
2	2.5mm seamless hollow gold-filled beads
33	43mm seamless hollow silver beads
1	4mm seamless hollow silver bead
1	4mm seamless hollow gold-filled bead
2	silver crimp beads
2	gold-filled crimp covers
1	silver gold toggle clasp
20"	of beading wire

DESIGNING WITH OTHER BEADS

USING OTHER MATERIALS WITH SILVER AND GOLD

Silver and gold are can be combined with an endless range of other components. Indeed, it is fair to say that almost all jewelry uses silver and gold in one form or another, even if only for a clasp or a spacer, and even if it is only cheap plate or imitation color.

But when you are making jewelry with real silver and real gold, the other materials must be of a certain quality. Not just any old bead can share the stage with precious metal. The designs in this chapter introduce you to some of the materials, shapes, and colors of beads that enhance the look of gold and silver jewelry. The materials lists of each design provides enough description for you to be able to find not just the silver and gold but all of the complementary beads, whether at your local bead store or from a mail order/Internet supplier. If there are occasions when you have trouble finding the exact match, don't be afraid to substitute similar beads of equal quality.

For gems, the choice whether to combine with silver or gold depends primarily on the color of the stone. Try to select gemstones that complement and enhance the color values of the precious metal. This is very much a matter of personal taste, but in general, if a gemstone has a strong reddish tone, it is likely to go better with gold, whereas black and gray tones work better with silver.

In all designs it is essential to create a sense of harmony among the individual components. For a jewelry designer this means trying to balance size, color, shape, and texture.

Size is a primary consideration. Do you want the precious metal to simply set off the gems, or do you want it and the other beads to command equal attention? You can easily achieve a sense of proportion by making all the beads a similar size, but equally effective is using several smaller beads to counterbalance each large bead.

Shape and texture are also important. A complex shape or pattern is bound to win more attention than a plain round bead. Texture comes to the forefront when set alongside a smooth surface.

COMBINE WITH GOLD

Silver

High quality gemstones

Other materials of high value

COMBINE WITH GOLD-FILLED AND VERMEIL

Silver

Medium value gemstones

Items of artistic value or personal value

COMBINE WITH SILVER

Gold, vermeil, and gold-filled

All gemstones

Glass crystal (such as Swarovski)

Fine quality lamp glass beads

Items of artistic value or personal value

Color plays a large role in the equation. Bright, vivid colors simply attract the eye more than those that are pale and subdued.

However you achieve your own harmonious look, precious metal should always be treated with due respect. Combining it with cheap materials does not enhance the value of the other beads, it just makes them look out of place. And they make the gold or silver look less valuable than it is. Even the simplest band of silver or gold possesses a degree of dignity and elegance. Whatever you add must, at a minimum, maintain those inherent qualities.

GEMSTONES THAT GO BETTER WITH GOLD

Garnet (including spessartine and hessonite)	Morganite
	Citrine
	Brandy quartz
Rhodochrosite	Amber
Coral (red)	Hessonite
Rose quartz	Carnelian
Pink sapphire	Opal
Pink tourmaline	

GEMSTONES THAT GO BETTER WITH SILVER

Black onyx	Coral (black)
Labradorite	Obsidian
Hematite	Jet

GEMSTONES THAT GO EQUALLY WELL WITH EITHER SILVER OR GOLD

Diamond	Tanzanite
Pearl	Green garnet
Iolite	(grossular)
Sapphire	Peridot
Blue topaz	Emerald
Kyanite	Chrome diopside
Lapis lazuli	Clear topaz
Turquoise	Rainbow moonstone
Aquamarine	
Amethyst	

NOTE

The more expensive the gem, the more likely it is to be better paired with gold, whether the usual yellow variety or white, rose, or green gold.

12.
BRUSHED SILVER AND AQUAMARINE

THIS NECKLACE SHOWS ANOTHER WAY OF BALANCING BEADS
SO THAT NEITHER ONE DOMINATES THE OTHER. THE BRUSHED
SILVER BEADS ARE CONSIDERABLY SMALLER THAN THE LARGE
AQUAMARINE BEADS, BUT RATHER THAN PLAYING THE ROLE OF
SPACERS, THE SILVER BEADS SHOW UP THE BIGGER BEADS BY
ADDING AN INTRIGUING DESIGN AND SURFACE TEXTURE THAT
IS EQUAL TO THE LARGER, PLAINER GEMS.

1. Start the necklace by threading on a crimp. Pass the beading
   wire through the ring of one half of the clasp back through the
   crimp. Make sure that the beading wire is tight around the ring
   and squeeze the crimp shut. Add a 5mm silver bead to cover the
   tail of the beading wire and cut.

2. Add an X bead and an aquamarine bead. Repeat this pattern
   twenty times and then add a final X bead.

3. Add the other 5mm bead. Bring the beading wire through the
   ring of the other side of the clasp and back through the crimp
   and round bead. Tighten the necklace so that all the beads fit
   snugly. Close the crimp and snip off any remaining beading wire.
   Add the crimp covers.

TOOLS
Wire Cutters, Crimping Pliers

MATERIALS
- 2 silver crimp beads
- 20" of .018 beading wire
- 1 silver stardust toggle clasp
- 2 5mm brushed silver beads
- 22 6mm by 8mm brushed silver X-shaped double-ended bead caps (each of the four sides forms an X)
- 21 12mm or 14mm round aquamarine beads
- 2 silver crimp covers

13.
SILVER AND JASPER

FINDING THE RIGHT BALANCE BETWEEN PRECIOUS METAL AND GEMSTONES CAN BE ACHIEVED IN MANY WAYS. HERE THE WIDTH OF THE RONDELS IS GREATER THAN THE JASPER BEADS, AND THIS CHANGES THEM FROM MERE SPACERS INTO EQUAL PARTNERS. NEITHER THE SILVER NOR THE JASPER DOMINATES, LEAVING THE EYE FREE TO ADMIRE EACH EQUALLY.

BLACK OR DARK JASPER HAS LONG BEEN USED TO TEST FOR GOLD CONTENT. AN ALLOY OF GOLD AND SILVER WAS RUBBED ON THE STONE AND THE COLOR OF THE MARK IT LEFT WOULD TELL THE PURITY OF THE GOLD TO WITHIN ONE PART IN A HUNDRED. THIS TYPE OF ROCK WAS CALLED A TOUCHSTONE, GIVING US OUR CURRENT WORD FOR A STANDARD OR CRITERION.

1. Start the necklace by threading on a crimp. Pass the beading wire through the ring of one half of the clasp and back through the crimp. Make sure that the beading wire is tight around the ring and squeeze the crimp shut. Add two 3mm silver round beads to cover the tail of the beading wire and cut. Add a 4mm silver bead and a 7mm silver bead.

2. Thread on a 15mm silver rondel and a jasper bead. Repeat this pattern twenty-six times or until the necklace is the right length for your neck.

3. Add a final silver rondel, a 7mm round silver bead, a 4mm round silver bead, and two 3mm round silver beads.

4. Add the remaining crimp bead and bring the beading wire through the ring of the other side of the clasp and back through the crimp and last silver round bead. Tighten the necklace so that all the beads fit snugly against each other. Close the crimp and snip off any remaining beading wire. Add the crimp covers.

TOOLS
Wire Cutters, Crimping Pliers

MATERIALS

2	silver crimp beads
20"	of .018 beading wire (This necklace is heavy and the thicker beading wire will be stronger.)
1	silver toggle clasp
4	3mm seamless hollow silver round beads
2	4mm seamless hollow silver round beads
2	7mm seamless hollow silver round beads
28	15mm silver rondels with large (6mm) holes
27	12mm Arizona jasper round beads
2	silver crimp covers

14.
SILVER AND TURQUOISE

THIS PATTERN IS SOMEWHAT RANDOM SO FEEL FREE TO VARY INGREDIENTS: YOU CAN USE OTHER STONES OR SILVER BEADS WHILE MAINTAINING THE RELATIVE SIZE PROPORTIONS. THE MATERIALS WILL MAKE ROUGHLY A SIXTY-TWO INCH ROPE LENGTH.

1. Start the necklace by threading on a crimp. Pass the beading wire through the ring of one half of the clasp back through the crimp. Make sure that the beading wire is tight around the ring and squeeze the crimp shut. Add two silver round beads to cover the tail of the beading wire and cut.

2. Add another silver round bead (s), a tube (t), s, carnelian 3mm (c3), silver chip (sc), turquoise nugget (nugget), sc, c3, s, t, black onyx 2mm (b2), silver three-side bead (tri), bo, t, turquoise 2-mm (t2), c3, s, silver bee's wing (bw), s, t2, t, t2, t, t2, s, tri, s, t, s, sc, nugget, sc, s, st, t2, s, c3, tri, c3, s, t2, t, green onyx 2mm (g2), nugget, g2, t, s, c3, s, t, t2, bw, t2, t, s, silver daisy (d), s, d, s, d, s, t, c2, tri, t2, t, s, sc, nugget, sc, s, sc, nugget, sc, s, sc, nugget, sc, s, t, g2, t, t2, bw, s, s, s, tri, s, s, s, t, t2, s, t2, tri, c3, t, t2, sc, t2, sc, t2, ts, t, t2, fish, s, c3, s, ts, b2, nugget, b2, tri, b2, t, s, sc, c3, sc, s, ts, t2, tri, t2, s, ts, nugget, sc, c3, sc, nugget, sc, c3, sc, nugget s, t, s, s, s, t, t2, c3, t2, t, s, s, s, s, t, t2, bw, t2, t, s, c3, s, c3, s, nugget, s, tri, c3, t2, t, t2, t, s, tri, s, t, s, sc, nugget, sc, s, t, c3, t, t2, s, t2, d, c3, s, t, t2, tri, s, t, t2, t, t2, t, t2, t, s, nugget, s, t, s, t, s, c3, tri, s, t2, s, t, b2, nugget, b3, t, t2, sc, t, c3, d, c3, t, t2, tri, t2, t, s, nugget, s, nugget, s, nugget, s, t, t2, bw, t2, c2, t, c2, c3, t, t2, tri, t2, c3, t2, t, t2, t, t2, t, t2, fish, t2, c3, t2, t, s, nugget, s, tri, s, t, c3, s, t, t2, tri, t2, t, s, s, s, tri, s, s, s, t, t2, tri, t2, t2, t, c3, sc, nugget, sc, nugget, t, t2, bw, t2, t, b2, tri, b2, t, s, nugget, s, t, t2, tri, t2t, c3, t, t2, s, c3, tri, c3, s, t2, t, s, nugget, s, c3, s, s, and s.

3. Add the remaining crimp bead and bring the beading wire through the ring of the other side of the clasp and back through the crimp and last silver round bead. Tighten the necklace so that all the beads fit snugly against each other. Close the crimp and snip off any remaining beading wire. Add the crimp covers.

TURQUOISE AND SILVER ARE A CLASSIC PARTNERSHIP. ALTHOUGH STRONGLY ASSOCIATED IN MODERN TIMES WITH THE JEWELRY OF THE SOUTHWESTERN UNITED STATES, THE COMBINATION HAS BEEN USED FOR THOUSANDS OF YEARS. TURQUOISE IS FRENCH FOR TURKISH, A NAME THAT RECALLS THE ROUTE THAT STONES FROM ANCIENT PERSIAN MINES TOOK TO REACH EUROPE. TODAY TURQUOISE DEPOSITS ARE FOUND IN MANY COUNTRIES AND OFFER A RANGE OF COLOR FROM SKY BLUE TO PALE GREEN.

TOOLS
Wire Cutters, Crimping Pliers

MATERIALS

2	silver crimp beads
66"	of beading wire
1	Thai silver toggle clasp
1	4mm silver seamless hollow round bead
85	2.5mm silver seamless hollow round beads
64	13mm silver curved tube beads
31	3mm carnelian round beads
23	4mm (approximately) Thai silver "chip" beads
19	12mm (approximately) turquoise nugget beads
68	2mm mixed stone round beads (mostly turquoise) (I have used 2 carnelian, 55 turquoise, 9 black onyx and 2 green onyx.)
21	4mm Thai silver three-sided beads
6	3mm by13mm Thai silver "bee's wing" beads
5	3mm silver double daisy spacer beads
2	22mm Thai silver "fish" beads
2	silver crimp bead covers

15.
SILVER AND PEARLS

THESE FRESHWATER PEARLS ARE DYED GRAY AND THEN
POLISHED TO PRODUCE A STEELY SURFACE COVERED WITH
IRIDESCENT REFLECTIONS. THEY ARE A PERFECT MATCH FOR
SILVER AND HAVE AN INTRIGUING METALLIC LOOK WHILE
RETAINING THE MINERAL FEEL OF A GEMSTONE.

1. Start the necklace by threading on a crimp. Pass the beading
   wire through the ring of one half of the clasp and back through
   the crimp. Make sure that the beading wire is tight around the
   ring and squeeze the crimp shut. Add two 3mm silver round
   beads to cover the tail of the beading wire and cut. Add a 5mm
   round bead.

2. Now thread on a double-sided bead cap and a pearl. Repeat this
   pattern forty times or until the necklace is the right length for
   your neck.

3. Add a final bead cap, a 5mm round silver bead, and two 3mm
   round silver beads.

4. Add the remaining crimp bead and bring the beading wire
   through the ring of the other side of the clasp and back through
   the crimp and last silver round bead. Tighten the necklace so
   that all the beads fit snugly against each other. Close the crimp
   and snip off any remaining beading wire. Add the crimp covers.

TOOLS
Wire Cutters, Crimping Pliers

MATERIALS

2	silver crimp beads
20"	of beading wire
1	silver toggle clasp
4	3mm seamless hollow silver round beads
2	5mm seamless hollow silver round beads
42	5mm double-sided silver granulated bead caps
41	7mm dyed and polished nearly round freshwater pearls (about 2/3 of a 16" strand)
2	silver crimp covers

16.
SILVER AND BLACK ONYX

THE COMBINATION OF SILVER AND BLACK CREATES AN ELEGANT LOOK—AT ONCE GLAMOROUS AND SERIOUS. THIS APPEARANCE IS ALSO HELPED BY THE ANTIQUED LINES ON THE DISCS, GIVING THEM A MODESTY THAT TONES DOWN THE LARGE AMOUNT OF SILVER THEY DISPLAY. ALTHOUGH THIS PIECE IS DESIGNED TO IMPRESS, NO ONE CAN ACCUSE THE WEARER OF BEING TOO SHOWY.

1. Start the necklace by threading on a crimp. Pass the beading wire through the ring of one half of the clasp back through the crimp. Make sure that the beading wire is tight around the ring and squeeze the crimp shut. Add two silver round beads to cover the tail of the beading wire and cut.

2. Now thread on two black onyx beads, a silver round, five onyx beads, and another silver round.

3. Add two black onyx beads, a silver round, a disc-shaped pendant bead, and another silver round. Repeat this pattern twenty times. Add two onyx beads, a silver round, five onyx, a silver round, two onyx, and another two silver rounds.

4. Add the remaining crimp bead and bring the beading wire through the ring of the other side of the clasp and back through the crimp and last silver round bead. Now tighten the necklace so that all the beads fit snugly against each other. Close the crimp and snip off any remaining beading wire. Add the crimp covers.

TOOLS
Wire Cutters, Crimping Pliers

MATERIALS

2	silver crimp beads
20"	of beading wire
1	silver antiqued toggle clasp
50	3mm seamless hollow silver round beads
58	4mm black onyx round beads
21	12mm Thai silver antiqued disc-shaped pendant beads
2	silver crimp covers

17.
SILVER AND APATITE NECKLACE

SILVER BEADS COME IN AN EXTRAORDINARY VARIETY OF SHAPES. NEW DESIGNS ARE BEING CREATED ALL THE TIME BY ARTISANS AND JEWELRY DESIGNERS AROUND THE WORLD. HANDCRAFTED IN NORTHERN THAILAND, THESE DELIGHTFUL SWIRL SHAPES SOMEHOW MANAGE TO APPEAR BOTH CONTEMPORARY AND TRADITIONAL. THE SOLID SILVER OF THE SWIRL BEADS IS EMPHASIZED BY THE SMALL SILVER NUGGET BEADS, GIVING THE NECKLACE A WEIGHTY AND SUBSTANTIAL APPEARANCE. THE APATITE BEADS ACT MORE AS SPACERS TO FRAME THE SILVER, WHICH IS THE REAL STAR OF THE DESIGN.

TOOLS
Wire Cutters, Crimping Pliers

MATERIALS
- 2 silver crimp beads
- 20" of beading wire
- 1 silver toggle clasp
- 96 4mm (approximately) silver nugget beads
- 62 4mm round apatite beads
- 23 10mm by 13mm flat disk Thai silver "swirl" beads
- 2 silver crimp bead covers

1. Start the necklace by threading on a crimp. Pass the beading wire through the ring of one half of the clasp back through the crimp. Make sure that the beading wire is tight around the ring and squeeze the crimp shut.

2. Thread on three silver nugget beads, one apatite bead, three nugget beads, three apatite beads, three nugget beads, one apatite bead, three nugget beads, and three apatite beads.

3. Add three silver nugget beads, one apatite bead, one silver swirl bead, and one apatite bead. Repeat this pattern twenty-two times.

4. Add three nugget beads, three apatite beads, three nugget beads, one apatite bead, three nugget beads, three apatite beads, three nugget beads, one apatite bead, three nugget beads, and a crimp. Bring the beading wire through the ring of the other side of the clasp and back through the crimp and round bead. Tighten the necklace so there are no spaces between the beads. Close the crimp and snip off any remaining beading wire. Add the crimp bead covers.

18.
VERMEIL, PEARLS, AND AQUAMARINE

THIS KIND OF DESIGN IS AN EXCELLENT WAY TO USE THE LEFTOVER BEADS FROM PREVIOUS PROJECTS OR TO DISPLAY INDIVIDUAL BEADS THAT YOU FOUND IRRESISTIBLE DURING YOUR LATEST BEAD SHOPPING EXPEDITION. MAKE SURE WHEN ADDING THE CHARMS TO ATTACH THEM ALL TO THE SAME SIDE OF THE CHAIN.

1. Start by making the aqua, pearl, and vermeil bead charms ready to dangle off the chain. Use the 2.5mm round beads and the daisy spacer beads to top and tail the dangle, but mix them to make several variations—with a daisy at the bottom and a round at the top, a daisy or a round top and bottom, or even a round and a daisy combination. Refer to the picture for guidance. All the dangles are made using the same technique: Starting with a 2" headpin, add a 2.5mm round or a daisy, or both. Then add one principal bead (aquamarine, vermeil, or pearl). Add the topping daisy or 2.5mm round. To see how they look, you can put all the beads on the headpins and lay them side-by-side before making the loops. That way, you can change any arrangements you don't like. When you are satisfied that all the dangles look good, cut the headpins so that about $^5/_8$" remains above the beads. Use your round-nosed pliers to make a wire-wrapped loop.

2. Lay the charms out in a line and arrange them in a random but balanced manner. Cut a 26" length of chain. Five inches from the beginning of the chain, add your first charm using your 3.5mm gold-filled jump rings. Every other loop, attach a charm.

3. With the leftover 3" length of chain, add one charm hanging from the bottom. On the next loop, add one charm on either side of the chain. Add a charm on the fourth and fifth loops.

4. Add a 3.5mm jump ring to the other end of the 3" chain and attach it to the 6mm heavy gauge jump ring. Attach the same 6mm jump ring to the end of the 26" length of chain and the loop of the lobster clasp. Close all the jump rings.

TOOLS
Round-Nosed Pliers, Flat-Nosed Pliers, Wire Cutters

MATERIALS

11	10mm by 12mm to 25mm by 13mm faceted aqua drops
11	9mm by 9mm potato pearls
17	assorted vermeil and gold-filled charms and seamless hollow round beads
54	2.5mm gold-filled seamless hollow round beads
30	4mm vermeil daisy spacer beads
37	2" vermeil headpins with ball tips
29"	of 7mm by 6mm gold-filled flat cable chain
39	3.5mm gold-filled jump rings
1	6mm 19-gauge gold-filled jump ring
1	22mm vermeil lobster clasp

NOTE
Before starting this necklace, you will need to read how to make a wire-wrapped loop in the Jewelry Techniques section.

19.
GREEN AND GOLD

ALTHOUGH WE OFTEN WANT TO PLAY UP THE WARM, REDDISH HUES OF GOLD, OTHER ASPECTS OF ITS CHARACTER CAN BE EQUALLY CHARMING. GREEN BRINGS OUT A COMPLETELY DIFFERENT SIDE OF GOLD, A LITTLE COOLER AND MORE DISCREET, BUT JUST AS BEAUTIFUL. HERE, SMOOTH NUGGETS OF GREEN PREHNITE COMPLEMENT THE HOLLOW GOLD NUGGETS IN BOTH COLOR AND SHAPE. THE BEADS ARE KNOTTED ON A PALE GREEN SILK THREAD, WHICH FURTHER ENHANCES THE LOOK OF THE GEMSTONE.

1. Read the instructions in Jewelry Techniques for stringing on silk and using basket bead tips. Attach one part of the clasp.

2. Knot on a 3mm gold bead and then, knotting between each bead, add three prehnite beads, one large gold bead, two prehnite beads, one large gold bead, one prehnite bead, one large gold bead, two prehnite beads, one large gold bead, one prehnite bead, one large gold bead, three prehnite beads, one large gold bead, one prehnite bead, one large gold bead, two prehnite beads, and one 3mm gold bead. Remember to knot between all the beads, making sure there are no gaps between the knots and the beads. Some of the knots might slip inside the large holes of the gold beads, but this does not matter. Try the necklace for length. (You can add another prehnite bead if necessary.)

3. Attach the bead tip and the other half of the clasp.

TOOLS
Awl, Flat-Nosed Pliers

MATERIALS
54" of pale green silk thread size F

2 14 karat gold basket bead tips

1 18 karat gold toggle clasp with chain

2 3mm 18 karat gold nugget beads

15 prehnite smooth nugget-shaped beads about 11mm wide and varying from 12mm to 16mm long

7 23mm by 12mm hollow 18 karat gold nugget-shaped beads

20.
COLORS OF ANCIENT EGYPT

MANY YEARS AGO I HAD THE GOOD FORTUNE TO VISIT TO THE EGYPTIAN MUSEUM IN CAIRO. I WAS AMAZED TO SEE 3,000-YEAR-OLD JEWELRY LOOKING AS IF IT COULD BE TAKEN FROM THE CASE AND WORN TO A SOPHISTICATED PARTY IN NEW YORK. THAT THE MATERIALS LOOKED FRESH DID NOT SURPRISE ME, FOR THEY WERE ALL TIMELESS GOLD AND GEMSTONES. BUT THE ENTIRELY "MODERN" SENSE OF COLOR WAS UNEXPECTED AND GAVE ME A FEELING OF EMPATHY WITH THESE ANCIENT DESIGNERS.

1. Thread on a crimp. Pass the beading wire through the ring of one half of the clasp back through the crimp. Be sure that the wire is tight around the ring and squeeze the crimp shut. Add a 2mm gold round bead to cover the tail of the wire and cut.

2. Because this asymmetrical necklace has a random order, refer to the picture for guidance threading on the beads, or create your own arrangement. It is important, however, that the five turquoise beads at the bottom are placed symmetrically and the three top-drilled turquoise beads are separated equally. In order to achieve this, check the length around your neck when you have reached 9". If it seems that another 1/2" will bring the necklace to the desired center point on your neck, add one of the smaller top-drilled beads, a 2mm round bead, a daisy spacer bead, another 2mm round bead, then the largest of the top-drilled beads, 2mm round bead, daisy spacer bead, 2mm round bead, and then the last of the top-drilled beads. Now add several gemstone and spacer beads until they are equal to the length of beads, separating the last turquoise bead from the first top-drilled bead. At that point add a turquoise bead and continue the random design with the rest of the beads, making sure that you reserve at least three smaller beads for the very end of the necklace.

3. Add the remaining crimp bead and bring the beading wire through the ring of the other side of the clasp and back through the crimp and last two or three beads. Tighten the necklace so that all the beads fit snugly against each other. Close the crimp and snip off any remaining beading wire. Add the crimp covers.

TOOLS
Wire Cutters, Crimping Pliers

MATERIALS

- 2 gold-filled crimp beads
- 20" of gold-plated beading wire
- 1 18 karat gold toggle clasp
- 25 2mm 18 karat gold seamless hollow round beads
- 12 turquoise faceted nuggets approximately 10mm by 8mm
- 3 turquoise top-drilled faceted nuggets between 13mm and 17mm in length
- 35 3mm 18 karat gold daisy spacer beads
- 33 2mm by 2.5mm purple garnet faceted rondel beads
- 22 3mm by 4mm spessartine faceted rondel beads
- 18 3mm by 4mm ruby faceted rondel beads
- 13 7mm 18 karat gold faceted seamless hollow round beads with resin cores
- 6 6mm 18 karat gold faceted seamless hollow round beads with resin cores
- 1 3mm coral round bead
- 2 gold-filled crimp covers

21.
GOLD AND CORAL

GOLD AND CORAL GO TOGETHER BEAUTIFULLY, BUT THERE
ARE SERIOUS QUESTIONS ABOUT THE SUSTAINABILITY AND
ECOLOGICAL IMPACT OF GEM-QUALITY CORAL GATHERING. THE
CORAL USED IN THIS PIECE IS FROM AN OLD NECKLACE. IF YOU
HAVE TROUBLE FINDING CORAL BEADS OR DON'T WISH TO
ENCOURAGE NEW PRODUCTION, SMALL RUBY BEADS WOULD
DO JUST AS NICELY.

1. Start the necklace by threading on a crimp. Pass the beading
   wire through the ring of one half of the clasp back through the
   crimp. Make sure that the beading wire is tight around the ring
   and squeeze the crimp shut. Cut off the tail of the wire very
   close to the crimp.

2. Thread on twenty-nine coral beads, then a gold bead and a
   coral bead. Repeat this coral and gold bead pattern another
   forty-two times. Try the necklace around your neck for size
   and add or subtract beads as necessary.

3. Add a final gold bead and the remaining twenty-nine coral
   beads. Bring the beading wire through the ring of the other
   side of the clasp and back through the crimp. Now tighten the
   necklace so that all the beads fit snugly. Close the crimp and
   snip off any remaining beading wire close to the crimp. Add
   the crimp covers.

TOOLS
Wire Cutters, Crimping Pliers

Materials

2	gold-filled crimp beads
20"	of .013 beading wire (The holes in the coral beads are very small.)
1	18 karat gold hook-and-eye clasp
100	2mm round coral beads
44	4.5mm by 6.5mm 18 karat gold side-drilled oblong beads
2	gold-filled crimp covers

22.
BEE'S WINGS NECKLACE

SOLID BEADS CAN LOOK BIGGER THAN THEY ACTUALLY ARE. THIS DESIGN RELIES ON A SHAPE THAT RESEMBLES BEE'S WINGS— TWO DISCS ATTACHED TO A CENTRAL JOINT. USED IN A LINE, THE BEADS CREATE A BROAD BAND OF GOLD THAT WRAPS AROUND THE NECK. DEEP RED CARNELIAN BEADS USED AS SPACERS ENHANCE THE THICK, RICH RIBBON OF GOLD. THE COLOR BLENDS WITH THE RED HUES IN THE GOLD, AND THE FACETS MATCH ITS REFLECTION. IF YOU WERE TO USE A DIFFERENT COLOR GEMSTONE, IT WOULD LESSEN THE ILLUSION OF A LARGE QUANTITY OF GOLD.

1. Start the necklace by threading on a crimp. Pass the beading wire through the ring of one half of the clasp and back through the crimp. Make sure that the beading wire is tight around the ring and squeeze the crimp shut. Add a gold round bead to cover the tail of the beading wire and cut.

2. Thread on a carnelian bead and a "bee's wings" bead. Repeat this pattern fifty-four times or until the necklace is the length you wish. (Remember to try it around your neck to make sure.)

3. Add a final carnelian bead, a round bead, and a crimp. Bring the beading wire through the ring of the other side of the clasp and back through the crimp and round bead. Now tighten the necklace so that there are no spaces between the beads, close the crimp, and snip off any remaining beading wire. Add the crimp covers.

4. Using the headpin, add a carnelian bead, gold "bee's wings" bead, another carnelian bead, and a round gold bead. Use your round-nosed pliers to grip the headpin about $1/4$" above the bead. Make a loop, attach it to the ring of the clasp, and wrap the tail of the headpin between the bottom of the loop and the top of the bead. (See Wire Wrapping in Jewelry Techniques, page 129.)

TOOLS
Wire Cutters, Crimping Pliers, Round-Nosed Pliers

MATERIALS
2 gold-filled crimp beads

20" of beading wire

1 18 karat gold toggle clasp

3 2.5mm 18 karat gold-filled hollow seamless round beads

58 6mm faceted deep red carnelian beads

56 14mm 18 karat vermeil "bee's wings" beads

2 gold-filled crimp covers

1 1" gold-filled headpin with ball tip

EXAMINING THE NOBLE AND PRECIOUS METAL

Silver and gold are called "noble" metals, elegantly distinguishing them from metals that are merely base. Their "nobility" makes them immune from the ordinary corrosive stresses of nature. Because they are both rare and very desirable, they are also "precious" metals. There are several other noble metals such as platinum and palladium and even, in physicists' eyes, copper; but, silver and gold are the undisputed leaders of the group. Others may be part of the royal family, but gold and silver will always king and queen.

Gold and silver are the very foundation of the jeweler's art. Even though our designs are enriched by thousands of other materials, it is to the precious metals that we always return. Often they are the stars of our show, but even when they are not prominently featured, they are nearly always in the chorus, even if only as a modest clasp or humble earwire. Indeed, only a tiny percentage of jewelry scorns to use one of these wonderful metals or their imitations. Silver and gold are the truly universal materials of jewelry.

The reasons for this are found not in fashion but in the rare qualities of each of these metals; qualities which have been recognized and valued for thousands of years.

For the jeweler, silver and gold are brother and sister, a genetic match, alike in several delightful traits. They are, at once, both soft and strong. They can be hammered or bent into whatever shape the designer needs. They are extremely ductile and can be stretched into fine wires or beaten into thin sheets. Yet they have high tensile strength—which is to say they don't break—at least not unless you really try. They have a convenient melting point; low enough to make them easy to cast in molds, but high enough to ensure that your rings will not disappear if accidentally dropped beside the fireplace. But above all, they are extremely good-looking. Their extraordinary ability to reflect light makes them very, very shiny. They glitter and sparkle and proclaim to the world, "look at me!" What more could anyone want from a material? Is it too wicked to think that if men had the same qualities as precious metals, they might make perfect husbands?!

23.
VERMEIL AND TOURMALINE

NO MATTER HOW FLEXIBLE BEADING WIRE BECOMES, IT IS DOUBTFUL IT WILL EVER PRECISELY MATCH THE LOOK OF SILK. THE LIGHT WEIGHT OF THESE BEADS DEMANDS A DELICACY THAT ONLY SILK CAN PROVIDE. THE LOVELY VERMEIL BEADS TAKE THE CONCEPT OF HOLLOWNESS TO THE EXTREME-THE PERFORATIONS ADD INTEREST, BUT REDUCE WEIGHT AND THEREFORE COST. THE BEAUTIFUL TOURMALINE STICKS ARE PIECES OF SINGLE CRYSTALS WHOSE GREEN-BLUE COLOR CONTAINS TRACES OF YELLOW, WHICH BLENDS PERFECTLY WITH THE GOLD. USING TURQUOISE-COLORED SILK ENHANCES THE LOOK OF THE GEMS.

TOOLS
Beading Needle, Awl, Scissors, Flat-Nosed Pliers

Materials

2	yards of #83 turquoise silk thread, size F
2	gold-filled basket bead tips
169	green tourmaline sticks approximately 3mm wide and 5mm to 10mm long (A 16" strand will leave enough extra sticks for a pair of earrings)
18	3mm gold-filled seamless hollow round beads
9	12mm vermeil hollow round beads with perforated star pattern
1	vermeil toggle clasp

1. Read the instructions in Jewelry Techniques for stringing on silk thread and basket bead tips. Note that in this design you are not going to knot between every bead, but between groups of beads as outlined in step 2 below. Start the necklace by threading a beading needle and making a knot at the end of the doubled thread. Following the instructions in Jewelry Techniques (page 126), add one of the basket bead tips.

2. Add five green tourmaline sticks and make a knot. Use your awl to make sure that the knot is tight against the beads. Now add three sticks and knot (always using the awl to make sure that the knots keep the beads tight against each other), another five sticks and knot, another three sticks and knot, and another five sticks and knot.

3. Add a 3mm gold-filled bead, then a 12mm vermeil bead, another 3mm bead, five tourmaline sticks and knot, three sticks and knot, and five sticks and knot. Repeat this pattern eight times.

4. Add five tourmaline sticks and knot, three sticks and knot, five sticks and knot, three sticks and knot, and another five sticks and knot.

5. And one more knot and then the other basket bead tip. Attach the toggle clasp to the bead tips.

24.
GOLD AND CUBIC ZIRCONIA

CUBIC ZIRCONIA, OR CZ, AS IT IS COMMONLY KNOWN, IS A LABORATORY-CREATED GEMSTONE THAT COMES IN A LARGE RANGE OF COLORS. IT WORKS WELL WITH GOLD, NOT JUST FOR THE COLOR BUT BECAUSE IT, LIKE GOLD, IS AN EXTRAORDINARILY DENSE AND HEAVY MATERIAL. THE UNUSUAL WEIGHT OF THE CZ ADDS TO THE NECKLACE AND MAKES IT FEEL AS IF THE GOLD LEAVES WERE SOLID INSTEAD OF HOLLOW.

1. Start the necklace by threading on a crimp. Pass the beading wire through the ring of one half of the clasp back through the crimp. Make sure that the beading wire is tight around the ring and squeeze the crimp shut.

2. Thread on a cubic zirconia bead and a gold bead. Repeat this pattern another twenty-four times. Try the necklace around your neck for size and add or subtract beads as necessary.

3. Add a final cubic zirconia bead. Bring the beading wire through the ring of the other side of the clasp and back through the crimp and round bead. Now tighten the necklace so that all the beads fit snugly. Close the crimp and snip off any remaining beading wire. Add the crimp covers.

TOOLS
Wire Cutters, Crimping Pliers

MATERIALS
- 2 gold-filled crimp beads
- 20" of gold-plated beading wire
- 1 18 karat gold toggle clasp
- 26 4mm red cubic zirconia faceted round beads
- 25 10mm by 6mm 18 karat gold hollow leaf-shaped beads
- 2 gold-filled crimp covers

25.
VERMEIL AND TOURMALINE EARRINGS

EARRINGS ARE EASY TO DESIGN AND QUICK TO CONSTRUCT. EVEN WITH ONLY A FEW MINUTES TO SPARE, I CAN THROW TOGETHER A PAIR OF EARRINGS TO MATCH THE DRESS I AM ABOUT TO WEAR THAT EVENING. I LET MY EYES PASS OVER THE BITS AND PIECES OF JEWELRY COMPONENTS THAT LITTER THE FLAT SURFACES OF MY STUDIO AND SELECT A FEW BEADS. IN A COUPLE OF MOMENTS, I HAVE THEM ON A HEADPIN: I MAKE A LOOP, ATTACH AN EARWIRE, AND HOLD UP A PERFECTLY FINISHED PIECE OF JEWELRY. OF COURSE, EARRINGS ARE SOMETIMES FAR MORE COMPLEX AND REQUIRE A GREAT DEAL MORE TIME TO CONSTRUCT, BUT IN GENERAL, THEY ARE THE QUICKEST ROUTE TO INSTANT GRATIFICATION.

1. Read the instructions in Jewelry Techniques for stringing on silk thread and basket bead tips. Thread a beading needle with nine inches of the thread. Double it and make a knot at the end of the doubled thread. Following the instructions in Jewelry Techniques (page 126), add one of the basket bead tips. Attach it to an ear-wire. Add a dab of hypo-cement (or clear nail polish) to the knot on the outside of the bead tip. Cut off the tail of the thread very close to the knot.

2. Add a 3mm round bead, then a 12mm vermeil bead. Now add twelve of the green tourmaline sticks and check that the earring is the right length for you. Add or subtract sticks to adjust the length, taking care that you have enough beads left over to make the other earring the same length as the first. Make a knot and use your awl to make sure that the knot is tight against the beads. Add a small dab of cement.

3. Complete the second earring as above, laying it against the other before the final knot and adjusting the number of tourmaline sticks to equalize the lengths.

TOOLS
Beading Needle, Awl, Scissors, Flat-Nosed Pliers, Hypo-Cement or Clear Nail Polish

MATERIALS

18 inches of #83 turquoise silk thread, size F

2 gold-filled basket bead tips

1 pair of gold-filled earwires

6 3mm gold-filled seamless hollow round beads

2 12mm vermeil hollow round beads with perforated star pattern

26 green tourmaline sticks approx. 3mm wide and 5mm to 10mm long (A 16" strand will leave enough extra sticks for a pair of earrings)

26.
GOLD AND TOPAZ EARRINGS

ALTHOUGH THE AMOUNT OF GOLD IN THE RESERVES OF NATIONAL GOVERNMENTS IS HIGHEST IN THE UNITED STATES AND THE EUROPEAN UNION, INDIA IS FIRST IN OVERALL OWNERSHIP OF GOLD. INDIAN WOMEN PLACE A LOT OF IMPORTANCE ON OWNING GOLD JEWELRY, AND THEY DESIRE EVER-GROWING COLLECTIONS OF NECKLACES, EARRINGS, BROOCHES, AND OTHER ACCESSORIES—ALL IN SOLID GOLD OF AT LEAST 22 KARATS. BUT BEFORE GASPING AT SUCH UNRESTRAINED VANITY, UNDERSTAND THAT IN MUCH OF ASIA, GOLD JEWELRY IS VIEWED MORE AS A SAVINGS ACCOUNT THAN A SIMPLE DECORATION. IT CAN BE FREELY EXCHANGED FOR MONEY AND IS CONSIDERED AS GOOD AS CASH IN THE BANK. IT DOES NOT EARN ANY INTEREST, BUT THERE IS GREAT FAITH IN ITS ABILITY TO MAINTAIN ITS VALUE AND APPRECIATE OVER TIME.

1. To each 1-inch headpin, add a gold faceted bead, a topaz bead, and another gold faceted bead. Make the beginnings of a wire-wrapped loop (see Jewelry Techniques, page 129). Attach this to the earwire and finish wrapping the tail of the headpin around the base of the loop.

2. To make the little dangles, add a faceted gold bead to each half-inch headpin. Make a simple loop and add another 2mm gold bead. Make a simple loop (see Jewelry Techniques), and before closing, attach the dangle to the loop of the earwire. Add four of these dangles to each earwire.

TOOLS
Round-Nosed Pliers, Flat-Nosed Pliers, Wire Cutters

MATERIALS
- 2 1" 18 karat gold headpins with ball tip
- 12 2mm 18 karat gold faceted beads
- 2 3mm faceted disc-shaped London blue topaz beads
- 1 pair of 18 karat gold earwires
- 8 1/2" 18 karat gold headpins with ball tip

27.
GOLD AND PREHNITE EARRINGS

GOLD AND A BEAUTIFUL GEMSTONE—SOMETIMES, ABSOLUTE
SIMPLICITY IS THE WAY TO GO!

1. Start the earring by adding a bead cap to your headpin. Add the
   prehnite oval nugget, another bead cap, and the 2.5mm round
   gold bead, and start making the beginning of a wire wrapped
   loop (see Jewelry Techniques).

2. Slip the loop onto the ring of the earwire and wrap the tail of the
   headpin around the base of the loop.

TOOLS
Round-Nosed Pliers

MATERIALS
4 2.5mm 18 karat gold bead caps

2 1" 18 karat headpins with ball tip

2 10mm by 13mm prehnite smooth
   oval nuggets

2 2.5mm 18 karat gold round beads

1 pair 18 karat gold earwires

28.
PEARL AND CORAL EARRINGS

THESE WONDERFUL DOUBLE-ENDED BEAD CAPS PRESENT
AN X DESIGN ON EACH OF FOUR SIDES. WHEN VIEWED
HORIZONTALLY, THEY LOOK LIKE A LITTLE BOW DECORATING
THE BEAUTIFUL LARGE PEARLS

1. Start the earring by adding a gold-filled cube bead to a headpin.
   Add a pearl, an X-shaped bead cap, a coral bead, another cube
   bead, and then start making the beginning of a wire-wrapped
   loop (see Jewelry Techniques).

2. Slip the loop onto the ring of the earwire and wrap the tail of
   the headpin around the base of the loop.

TOOLS
Round-Nosed Pliers, Flat-Nosed Pliers,
Wire Cutters

MATERIALS
4 2.5mm gold-filled cube beads

2 2" vermeil headpins with ball tip

2 8mm by 12mm rice-shaped freshwater
   pearls

2 6mm by 8mm vermeil X-shaped
   double-ended bead caps

2 5mm coral round beads

1 pair gold-filled earwires

NOTE
Before starting this pair of earrings, you need
to read how to make a wire-wrapped loop in
the Jewelry Techniques section.

29.
GOLD AND CRYSTAL EARRINGS

ANOTHER EXAMPLE OF HOW WELL FINE GLASS CAN GO WITH
VERMEIL, PARTICULARLY WHEN IT IS A COLOR WHICH SO SUBTLY
ENHANCES THE GOLDEN HUE OF THE OTHER 2 BEADS.

1. Start the earring by making all the little crystal dangles. Add to
    each $1/2$" headpin a crystal and a 2mm gold bead. Make a simple
    loop (see Jewelry Techniques, page 129).

2. To each earwire, add one of the remaining crystal beads and a
    3mm gold bead, then make a simple loop.

3. To each 2" headpin, add a 2.5mm gold bead, a 9mm gold
    bead, another 2.5mm bead, nine dangles, and a 3mm bead.
    Cut the headpin about $5/8$" above the last bead and make a
    wire-wrapped loop (see Jewelry Techniques, page 129). Attach
    this to the earwire by opening the loop of the earwire.

TOOLS
Round-Nosed Pliers, Flat-Nosed Pliers,
Wire Cutters

MATERIALS

18	$1/2$" vermeil headpins with ball tips
20	4.5mm Swarovski 5310 (simplicity) crystal Golden Shadow beads
18	2mm gold-filled seamless hollow round beads
1	pair gold-filled "add-on" earwires
2	3mm gold-filled seamless hollow round beads
2	2" vermeil headpins with ball tips
4	2.5mm gold-filled seamless hollow round beads
2	9mm gold-filled seamless hollow round beads

NOTE
Before starting this pair of earrings, you will
need to read how to make simple loops and
wire-wrapped loops in the Jewelry Techniques
section (page 129).

30.
PINK SAPPHIRE AND GOLD-FILLED NECKLACE

REDDISH TONES SEEM TO ENHANCE THE LOOK OF GOLD, INCREASING ITS IMPACT. THE PINK SAPPHIRES IN THIS SIMPLE DESIGN ADD RICH GLOW TO THE MODEST AND INEXPENSIVE GOLD-FILLED ROUND BEADS.

1. Start the necklace by threading on a micro-crimp. Pass the beading wire through the ring of one half of the clasp and back through the crimp. Add one 2mm by 2mm crimp and pass it over the micro-crimp. Make sure that the beading wire is tight around the ring and squeeze the crimps shut using the crimping pliers.

2. Thread on seven gold-filled beads and a pink sapphire bead. Add three gold-filled beads and a sapphire. Repeat this pattern twenty-five times or until the necklace is the length you wish. (Remember to try it around your neck to make sure.)

3. Add a final set of seven gold beads, a micro-crimp, and a 2mm by 2mm crimp. Bring the beading wire through the ring of the other side of the clasp and back through the crimp and round bead. Now tighten the necklace so there are no spaces between the beads. Close the crimp and snip off any remaining beading wire. Finish off by adding the crimp covers.

TOOLS
Wire Cutters, Crimping Pliers

MATERIALS

2 gold-filled micro-crimp beads

20" of .013 beading wire (Note: I have used .013 wire instead of .015 because of the very small hole size of the pink sapphires)

1 9mm round, gold filled box clasp

2 2mm by 2mm gold-filled crimps

92 2.5mm gold-filled seamless round beads

27 9mm by 9mm pink sapphire box-cut briolette

2 gold-filled crimp covers

31.
LONDON BLUE TOPAZ NECKLACE

CLEAR TOPAZ IS COMMONLY TREATED TO PRODUCE STUNNING SHADES OF BLUE. "LONDON" BLUE IS THE NAME FOR A MEDIUM TO DARK GRAYISH BLUE SOMETIMES DESCRIBED AS A LITTLE "INKY". IT IS A RICH AND DIGNIFIED COLOR WHICH GOES PERFECTLY WITH GOLD.

1. Start the necklace by threading on a crimp. Pass the beading wire through the ring of one half of the clasp back through the crimp. Make sure that the beading wire is tight around the ring and squeeze the crimp shut.

2. Thread on seven gold beads and a London blue topaz bead. Repeat this pattern twenty-one times or until the necklace is the length you wish. (Remember to try it around your neck to make sure.)

3. Add a final set of seven gold beads and a crimp. Bring the beading wire through the ring of the other side of the clasp and back through the crimp and round bead. Now tighten the necklace so there are no spaces between the beads. Close the crimp and snip off any remaining beading wire.

TOOLS
Wire Cutters, Crimping Pliers

MATERIALS

2	gold-filled micro-crimp beads
20"	of .013 beading wire
1	18 karat gold toggle clasp
154	2mm 18 karat gold faceted beads
21	8mm by 3mm faceted disc-shaped London blue topaz beads

NOTE:
Using the thinner .013 wire instead of .015 allows you to use a micro-crimp bead. Because this bead is almost invisible beside the little faceted beads, you can avoid using crimp covers. If you use .015 wire and regular crimps, you should add crimp covers.

32.
GOLD AND CUBIC ZIRCONIA BRACELET

MULTIPLE STRANDS OF TINY BEADS CREATE A WIDE BAND AND ARE MORE ECONOMICAL THAN USING LARGE GOLD BEADS.

1. Cut the beading wire into three 10" pieces. Divide the daisy spacer, round beads, and cubic zirconia beads into three equal parts, keeping the ratio of the colors of the CZ roughly even.

2. Put a piece of scotch tape around one end of a piece of the beading wire to prevent the beads falling off. Thread one set of beads onto the beading wire in a random pattern. Refer to the picture if you need guidance on color balance. When you have threaded on all the beads (approximately $6^{1}/_{2}$"), put another piece of tape or a clip on the other end to prevent the beads falling off.

3. Do the same with the next two pieces of beading wire, making sure that the length of beads on each of them is exactly the same as the first. Be sure the beads are all tightly together when you are comparing them.

4. Remove the tape. Thread a crimp onto one of the pieces and pass it through the top ring of one half of the clasp and back through the crimp. Make sure that the beading wire is tight around the ring and squeeze the crimp shut.

5. Remove the tape at the other end of the wire, thread on a crimp, and attach in the same way to the bottom ring of the other half of the clasp. Make sure all the beads are tightly together before closing the crimp. (Note: The two halves of a sliding clasp must be facing in opposite direction to fit together properly.)

6. Attach the second strand in the same way to the middle rings of the clasp, and then the third to remaining rings. In each case make sure the beads are snug and the lengths of the strands are roughly even. (It is unlikely that they will be exactly even, but a small difference in length will not be noticeable on your wrist.) Add the crimp covers.

TOOLS
Wire Cutters, Crimping Pliers, Tape

MATERIALS (7" BRACELET)

30"	of beading wire (preferably gold-plated)
101	4mm vermeil daisy spacer beads
69	2mm vermeil faceted rounds beads
120	3mm by 4mm multi-colored cubic zirconia (CZ) faceted rondel beads (a little less than a 16" strand of multi-colored CZ)
6	gold-filled crimps
1	vermeil 3 ring slide clasp
6	gold-filled crimp covers

33.
FACETED CUBIC ZIRCONIA AND GOLD-FILLED

ONE ADVANTAGE OF LABORATORY-MADE GEMSTONES IS THAT THEY CAN BE CREATED IN A BROAD RANGE OF COLORS AS IN THESE LOVELY CUBIC ZIRCONIA BEADS.

1. Start the necklace by threading on a crimp. Pass the beading wire through the ring of one half of the clasp back through the crimp. Make sure that the beading wire is tight around the ring and squeeze the crimp shut.

2. Start with one 2.5mm round gold-filled bead, then add D, CZ, D, CZ, D, CZ, CZ, CZ, D, D, D, CZ, FB, CZ, CZ, CZ, FB, FB, FB, CZ, CZ, D, CZ, D, CZ, D, CZ, D, CZ, FB, FB, D, CZ, D, FB, D, D, CZ, D, CZ, CZ, D, CZ,D, FB, FB, FB, CZ, CZ, Z, D, D, D, CZ, CZ, D, FB, D, CZ, D, CZ, CZ, CZ, FB, FB, FB, D, CZ, D, FB, CZ, D, CZ, FB, D, D, D, CZ, D, CZ, FB, D, CZ, D, CZ, D, CZ, CZ, CZ, CZ, D, FB, CZ, D, CZ, D, CZ, D, D, D, CZ, FB, FB, FB, D, CZ, D, CZ, CZ, D, CZ, FB, D, CZ, D, CZ, CZ, CZ, CZ, FB, CZ, D, D, D, FB, CZ, FB, D, CZ, CZ, D, CZ, FB, CZ, FB, CZ, FB, D, CZ, D, FB, CZ, CZ, CZ, CZ, FB, D, CZ ,D, CZ, CZ,CZ, FB, D, CZ, D, FB, CZ, D, D, CZ, FB, CZ, FB, D, CZ, CZ, D, CZ, D, CZ, D, CZ, CZ, CZ, FB, FB, FB, D, CZ, D, FB, FB, FB, D, CZ, CZ, CZ, D, CZ, D, D, D, CZ, D, CZ, FB, CZ, FB, D, CZ, D, CZ, CZ, CZ, D, D, CZ, D.

3. Add a final 2.5mm gold-filled bead. Add your crimp and pass the wire through the ring of the other half of the clasp. Bring the beading wire through the ring of the other side of the clasp and back through the crimp and round bead. Now tighten the necklace so that all the beads fit snugly. Close the crimp and snip off any remaining beading wire. Add the crimp covers.

TOOLS
Wire Cutters, Crimping Pliers

MATERIALS
72   4mm vermeil daisies
40   2.5 mm faceted gold filled beads
90   3 by 4mm faceted cubic Zirconia beads
 2   2.5mm gold filled beads
 2   gold-filled crimps
 2   gold-filled crimp covers
 1   vermeil toggle clasp
20"   of .015 beading wire

NOTE
The following is the key for this necklace.
CZ = cubic Zirconia, D = daisy, FB = faceted 2.5mm bead.

34.
SMALL IS BEAUTIFUL

JUST BECAUSE SOLID GOLD IS EXPENSIVE DOESN'T MEAN
YOU HAVE TO DEPRIVE YOURSELF. CLEVERLY USED, THE
TINIEST AMOUNT OF GOLD CAN PRODUCE A NECKLACE OF
MODEST RICHNESS THAT SPEAKS OF BOTH GOOD TASTE AND
DISCRETION. ALTHOUGH THERE ARE A LOT OF TINY GOLD
BEADS IN THIS CHOKER, THEIR TOTAL WEIGHT IS ONLY
ABOUT A TENTH OF AN OUNCE.

1. Start the necklace by threading on a crimp. Pass the beading
    wire through the ring of one half of the clasp back through the
    crimp. Make sure that the beading wire is tight around the ring
    and squeeze the crimp shut.

2. Now thread on a gemstone bead and a gold bead. Repeat this
    pattern until you have used all the beads or until the necklace
    is the right size for your neck. Look at the necklace from time to
    time to make sure that the alternating colors are well balanced.
    A random pattern should work well, but if your initial arrange-
    ment doesn't please you, just try a different one. Remember to
    finish off the pattern with a gemstone bead.

3. Bring the beading wire through the ring of the other side of
    the clasp and back through the crimp and round bead. Tighten
    the necklace so that all the beads fit snugly. Close the crimp
    and snip off any remaining beading wire. Add the crimp covers.

TOOLS
Wire Cutters, Crimping Pliers

MATERIALS (15" CHOKER)
2   gold-filled crimp beads
1   18 karat hook-and-eye clasp
20" of beading wire
104 2mm multi-stone round beads
     (about half a 16" strand)
102 2mm 18 karat gold cube beads
2   gold-filled crimp covers

NOTE
The little multi-stone beads can be bought
as a strand or you can use whatever 2mm
gemstones you choose. Some leftover
turquoise beads have been used here.

35.
SAPPHIRES AND GOLD

SPACER BEADS CAN BE AN INEXPENSIVE WAY OF DRESSING UP A NECKLACE WITH SOLID GOLD. IN THIS DESIGN THE LITTLE FACETED GOLD-FILLED BEADS PROVIDE THE GLITTER, AND THE DAISIES CARRY THE THEME THROUGHOUT THE WHOLE STRAND OF MULTI-COLORED SAPPHIRES.

1. Start the necklace by threading on a crimp. Pass the beading wire through the ring of one half of the clasp back through the crimp. Make sure that the beading wire is tight around the ring and squeeze the crimp shut. Add three gold faceted beads to hide the tail of the wire and cut.

2. Save three gold faceted beads for the end of the necklace and arrange the others in a manner pleasing to you. Refer to the picture on page 87 for guidance.

3. Once you are happy with the arrangement and the length of the necklace, add the final three gold faceted beads and a crimp. Pass the wire through the ring of the other half of the clasp. Bring the beading wire through the ring of the other side of the clasp and back through the crimp and two or three of the gold beads. Now tighten the necklace so that all the beads fit snugly. Close the crimp and snip off any remaining beading wire.

TOOLS
Wire Cutters, Crimping Pliers

MATERIALS

2	1mm gold-filled micro-crimps
20"	of .013 gold plated beading wire (The sapphire bead holes are very small)
1	18 karat gold lobster clasp
56	3mm 18 karat gold faceted beads
47	3mm 18 karat gold daisy beads
144	(approximately) 2mm by 4mm sapphire rondel beads (There will be enough left over from a 16" strand for a matching bracelet)

NOTE
There are no crimp covers available for micro-crimps, but the crimps add just a tiny speck of gold that is scarcely noticeable.

36.
KYANITE AND PRECIOUS METAL CLAY (PMC)

ALTHOUGH PMC IS MORE EXPENSIVE THAN SHEET OR WIRE, IT IS SO EASY TO WORK WITH THAT ENTHUSIASTIC DESIGNERS AROUND THE WORLD HAVE BEEN USING IT TO CREATE NEW AND EXCITING JEWELRY. THESE PMC SILVER BEADS WERE CREATED BY ONE OF OUR BEADWORKS DESIGNERS TO COMPLEMENT THE LOVELY KYANITE GEMSTONE SHAPES.

PRECIOUS METAL CLAY (PMC) IS A RECENT DEVELOPMENT IN THE HISTORY OF SILVER AND GOLD. IN THE LATE 1990s, A LARGE JAPANESE INDUSTRIAL COMPANY DEVELOPED A METHOD OF BINDING MICROSCOPIC PARTICLES OF SILVER OR GOLD INTO A MOIST, CLAY-LIKE MATERIAL. THE CLAY CAN BE EASILY MOLDED WITH NO SPECIAL TOOLS. WHEN FIRED IN A SMALL KILN, THE PARTICLES OF PRECIOUS METAL FUSE TOGETHER TO PRODUCE PURE SILVER OR 22 KARAT GOLD.

1. Start the necklace by threading your needle so that both ends of the silk meet. Now tie a knot, pull tight with your flat-nosed pliers, and make a second knot over the first knot. Cut close to the knot and apply a drop of hypo-cement. Add a picnic basket bead and, using your awl, make a knot after the picnic basket bead. (See Jewelry Techniques.)

2. Add one 2.5mm silver bead and one 3mm silver bead.

3. Add K, S, K, S, K, S, K, S, K, S, PMC, S, K, S, K, S, PMC, S, K, S, PMC, S, K, S, K, S, K, PMC, S, K, S, K, S, K, S, PMC, S, K, S, PMC, K, S, K, S, PMC, S, PMC, S, PMC, S, K, S, K, S, PMC, S, K, S, K, S, K, S, PMC, S, K, S, K, S, PMC, S, K, S, K, S, K, S, PMC, S, PMC, S, K, S, PMC, S, K, S, PMC, S, PMC, S, K, S, K, S, K, S, PMC, S, K, S, K, S, PMC, S, K, S, K, S, K, S, PMC, S, K, S, PMC, S, PMC, S, PMC, S, K, S, K, S, PMC, S, K, S, PMC, S, K, S, K, S, K, S, PMC, S, K, S, K, S, K, S, PMC, S, K, S, PMC, S, K, S, K, S, PMC, S, K, S, K, S, K, S, K, S, K.

4. Add the last 3mm silver beads, then a 2.5mm sterling silver bead. Make a knot with your awl. Put the needle through the bead tip. Using your awl, make another knot to fit inside the bead tip. Then make another knot, add a drop of hypo-cement or clear nail polish, and cut the thread.

5. Attach the toggle clasp using flat-nosed pliers to close the loops of the picnic basket bead tips around the clasp rings.

TOOLS

Wire Cutters or Scissors, Flat-Nosed Pliers, Awl, Hypo-Cement or Clear Nail Polish

MATERIALS

2	yards of size F light blue silk
1	size 10 twisted wire needle
2	sterling silver picnic basket bead tips
86	2.5mm silver round beads (S)
2	3mm silver round beads
56	11mm by 4mm kyanite flat drop beads (K)
29	11mm by 4mm to 16mm by 5mm PMC silver flat drop beads (PMC)
1	sterling silver toggle clasp

37.
SILVER, GOLD, AND JADE BRACELET

BRACELETS ARE OFTEN VIEWED FROM THE SIDE, ESPECIALLY BY
THE PERSON WHO IS WEARING THEM. THE LARGE BRUSHED
SILVER DISCS PERFORM WONDERFULLY FROM THIS PERSPECTIVE,
SHOWING A LARGE AREA OF PRECIOUS METAL AND REFLECTING
THE INTENSE GREEN OF THE JADE.

1. Start the bracelet by threading on a crimp. Pass the beading
    wire through the ring of one half of the clasp and back through
    the crimp. Make sure that the beading wire is tight around the
    ring and squeeze the crimp shut. Add a 6mm gold-filled round
    bead to cover the tail of the beading wire and cut.

2. Thread on a silver disc, a gold-filled 3mm bead, another disc,
    a jade bead, a disc, a jade bead, a disc, a jade bead, a 3mm
    round bead, a disc, a 3mm round bead, a disc, a 3mm round
    bead, a disc, a 3mm round bead, a jade bead, a disc, a jade
    bead, a disc, a jade bead, a 3mm round bead, a disc, a 3mm
    round bead, a disc, a 3mm round bead, a disc, a 3mm round
    bead, a jade bead, a disc, a jade bead, a disc, a 3mm round
    bead, a disc, and a 6mm round bead.

3. Add the remaining crimp bead and bring the beading wire
    through the ring of the other side of the clasp and back
    through the crimp and last silver round bead. Now tighten
    the bracelet so that all the beads fit snugly against each
    other. Close the crimp and snip off any remaining beading
    wire. Add the crimp covers.

4. To make the dangle, add a 3mm gold-filled round bead to the
    headpin, then a jade bead, a silver disc, and another 3mm
    gold-filled round bead. Cut the headpin to leave about $5/8$" above
    the last bead. See Jewelry Techniques to make a wire-wrapped
    loop. Start the loop and slip it onto the ring of the clasp. Close
    the loop and finish wrapping the wire around its base.

TOOLS
Wire Cutters, Crimping Pliers,
Round-Nosed Pliers, Flat-Nosed Pliers

MATERIALS (7" BRACELET)
2	silver crimp beads
12"	of .018 beading wire
1	silver spring ring clasp
2	6mm gold-filled seamless hollow round beads
12	3mm gold-filled seamless hollow round beads
16	2mm by 12mm brushed silver discs
9	12mm green jade beads
2	silver crimp covers
1	2" silver headpin

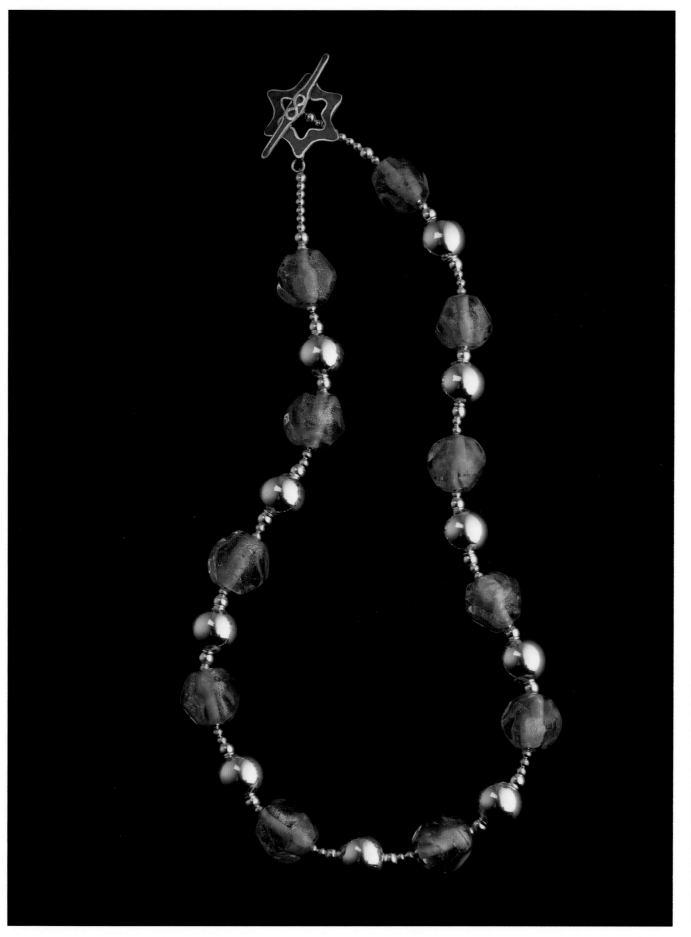

38.
SILVER AND DICHROIC GLASS

DICHROIC GLASS IS CREATED BY COATING METALLIC SALTS ONTO GLASS IN A VACUUM PROCESS. WHEN USED BY SKILLED LAMPWORK ARTISANS, IT CREATES BEADS WITH AN EXTRAORDINARY INTERNAL FIRE, SIMILAR TO THAT OF OPALS. IN THIS CASE, THE BEADS HAVE A SILVERY IRIDESCENCE, AS IF SILVER POWDER WERE TRAPPED INSIDE THE GLASS. BECAUSE THESE BEADS HAVE LARGE HOLES, THEY CAN SLIDE BACK AND FORTH OVER THE SMALL SILVER BEADS, WHICH GIVES THE NECKLACE A PLAYFUL QUALITY AND REALLY SHOWCASES THE BEAUTY OF THE DICHROIC GLASS.

1. Start the necklace by threading on a crimp. Pass the beading wire through the ring of one half of the clasp and back through the crimp. Make sure that the beading wire is tight around the ring and squeeze the crimp shut. Add two 2.5mm silver round beads to cover the tail of the beading wire and cut.

2. Add four more 2.5mm beads and then a 4mm bead followed by nine 2.5mm beads. Now add a dichroic bead so that it slides over the last eight silver beads.

3. Add a 4mm bead, a 10mm bead, another 4mm bead, and nine 2.5mm beads. Slip on a dichroic bead so that it slides of over the last eight silver beads. Repeat this pattern nine more times. Then add a 4mm bead and six more 2.5mm beads.

4. Add the remaining crimp bead and bring the beading wire through the ring of the other side of the clasp and back through the crimp and last silver round bead. Now tighten the necklace so that all the beads fit snugly against each other. Close the crimp and snip off any remaining beading wire. Add the crimp covers.

TOOLS
Wire Cutters, Crimping Pliers

MATERIALS
- 2 silver crimp beads
- 20" of .018 beading wire (I have used .018 here because the beads are fairly heavy. 015 would also work.)
- 1 silver and enamel toggle clasp
- 111 2.5mm silver seamless hollow round beads
- 22 4mm silver seamless hollow round beads
- 11 15mm dichroic glass nugget beads with a large 2.5mm to 3mm hole
- 10 10mm silver seamless hollow round beads
- 2 silver crimp bead covers

39.
SILVER-FOIL GLASS WITH STERLING SILVER DAISIES

SILVER IS AT THE HEART OF EACH OF THESE HAND-CRAFTED EUROPEAN GLASS BEADS. A LAYER OF PURE SILVER FOIL IS WRAPPED AROUND THE CORE OF THE BEAD BEFORE THE FINAL LAYER OF MOLTEN GLASS IS ADDED, GIVING A PARTICULAR RICHNESS AND REFLECTIVITY.

1. Start the necklace by threading on a crimp. Add six 3mm sterling silver beads and pass the beading wire through the ring of one half of the toggle and then back through the crimp, forming a loop. Squeeze the crimp shut and add a 3mm sterling silver bead.

2. Thread on a D, FB, D, FB, D, FB, D, FB, D, FB, 9D, FB, D, FB, D, FB, D, FB, D, FB, D, FB, 9D, FB, D, FB, D, FB, D, FB, D, FB, 9D, FB, D, FB, D, FB, D, FB, D, FB, D.

3. Add a 2.5mm sterling silver bead, a lampwork bead, a 2.5mm sterling silver bead, D, FB, D, and another 2.5mm sterling silver bead. Repeat this pattern three times Add another lampwork bead and a 2.5mm sterling silver bead. Continue with D, FB, D, FB, D, FB, D, FB, D, FB, 9D, FB, D, FB, D, FB, D, FB, D, FB, 9D, FB, D, FB, D, FB, D, FB, D, FB, 9D, FB, D, FB, D, FB, D, FB, D, FB, D.

4. Add a final 3mm sterling silver bead and a crimp. Bring the beading wire through the ring of the other side of the toggle clasp and back through the crimp and round bead. Tighten the necklace so that all the beads fit snugly. Close the crimp and snip off any remaining beading wire. Add the crimp covers.

TOOLS
Wire Cutters, Crimping Pliers

MATERIALS
- 2 sterling silver crimp beads
- 12 3mm sterling silver round beads
- 20" .015 beading wire
- 1 sterling silver toggle clasp
- 99 4mm sterling silver daisies (D)
- 45 3mm by 5mm assorted faceted semi-precious beads (iolite, green garnet, smoky quartz) (FB)
- 5 18mm by 23mm silver foil lampwork beads
- 6 2.5mm sterling silver round beads
- 2 sterling silver crimp covers

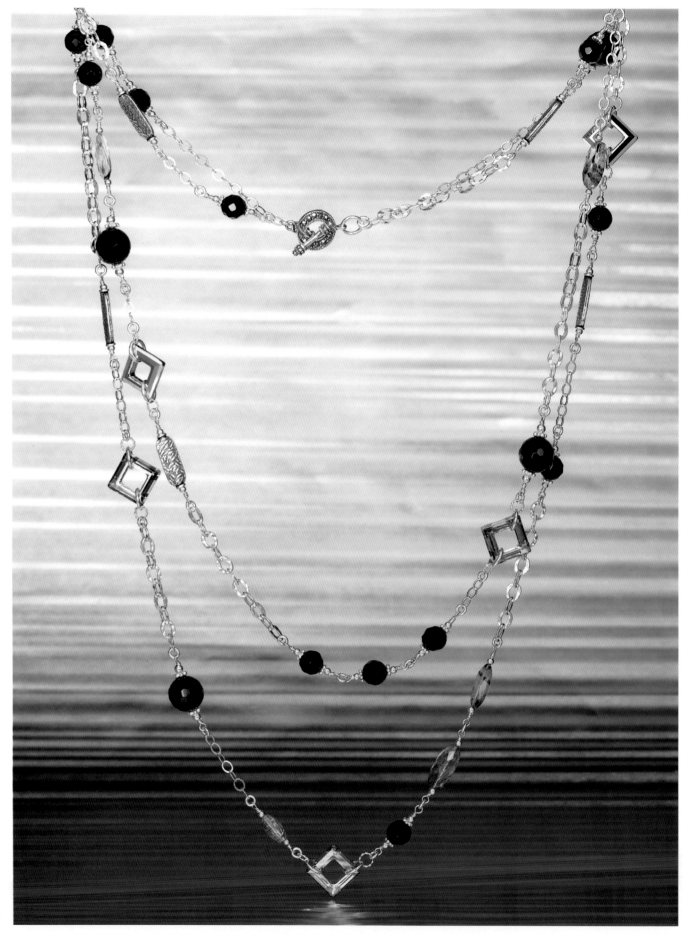

40.
SILVER CHAIN AND WIRE

THE SIMPLE ELEGANCE OF SILVER AND BLACK IS TRANSFORMED
HERE INTO AN EXTRAVAGANT DISPLAY. EACH TYPE OF CHAIN IS
AN INTEGRAL PART OF THE DESIGN RATHER THAN JUST A STRAND
LINKING THE WIRE-WRAPPED BEADS. THE RUTILATED QUARTZ
AND SQUARE SWAROVSKI CRYSTAL BEADS ADD THEIR OWN
DISTINCTIVE CHARACTER TO THE BASIC BLACK AND SILVER THEME.

1. Cut the wire into twelve pieces that are 2" long and fourteen
   pieces that are 2¹/₂" long. Use them to create wire-wrapped,
   double-ended pendants of all the beads (except the Swarovski
   squares) as follows:

2. (A) 2" wire, 3mm silver round, 5mm daisy, 14mm onyx, 5mm
   daisy, 3mm silver round

3. (B) 2¹/₂" wire, 2mm silver round, 4mm daisy, 8mm onyx, 4mm
   daisy, 2mm silver round

4. (C) 2¹/₂" wire, 2mm silver round, 19 7mm silver bead, 2mm silver
   round

TOOLS
Wire Cutters, Round-Nosed Pliers,
Flat-Nosed Pliers

MATERIALS

59"	of 22-gauge silver wire
8	3mm seamless hollow silver round beads
8	5mm silver daisy spacer beads
4	14mm faceted black onyx round beads
44	2mm seamless hollow silver round beads
22	4mm silver daisy spacer beads
5	19mm by 7mm silver antiqued rectangular beads
12	8mm faceted black onyx round beads.
5	faceted rutilated quartz oval beads 8mm wide and between 10mm and 16mm long
5	14mm by 14mm Swarovski crystal square (style 4439) beads
11	9mm silver 19-gauge jump rings
10	5mm silver twisted wire rings
13"	of silver cable chain with 5mm links (SC)
1	silver with marcasite toggle clasp
50	4mm silver 19-gauge jump rings
15"	of silver cable chain with flattened 7mm links (LC)

41.
SWAROVSKI CRYSTAL AND STERLING SILVER

HERE IS ANOTHER WAY OF USING SUPERB QUALITY GLASS WITH SILVER. THE CRYSTAL SQUARES ARE EQUALLY BALANCED WITH THE SILVER CHAIN TO PRODUCE A GLITTERING EFFECT.

1. Start the necklace by adding to the swivel clasp one 9mm jump ring to which a 1.75 inch piece of chain has been attached.

2. On the other end of the chain, add the 3.5mm jump ring to the twisted wire ring; then add the 9mm jump ring to the square Swarovski and the twisted wire ring.

3. Add another 9mm jump ring to the square ring and a twisted wire ring. Add the 3.5mm ring to the twisted wire ring and the next 1 inch section of chain. Repeat this step 3 more times.

4. At the middle of the necklace, once you have added the 3.5mm jump ring to the twisted wire ring, then add one 9mm jump ring to the Swarovski square. Take another 3.5mm jump ring that has been added to the previous twisted wire ring, and then add the next 1 inch section of chain. Repeat this pattern so that it duplicates the first half of the necklace.

5. Finish of the necklace with a single 9mm jump ring to which you will attach the swivel clasp when wearing.

TIP: WHEN OPENING AND CLOSING LARGE AND SMALL JUMP RINGS, IT IS HELPFUL TO HAVE TWO PAIR OF FLAT NOSE PLIERS ON HAND.

TOOLS
Wire Cutters, Wire Cutters, Flat-Nosed Pliers

MATERIALS
- 7 Swarovski Square Ring (4439) 14mm
- 15 9mm sterling silver jump rings 19 gauge
- 1 16mm sterling silver swivel clasp
- 13 4.5mm twisted wire sterling silver soldered rings
- 14 3.5mm heavy gauge s/s jump rings
- 9 .5 inches hammered 6 by 5-mm hammered s/s cable chain

42.
GOLD AND HANDMADE GLASS

ALTHOUGH "GEMSTONE" SOUNDS BETTER THAN "GLASS," THE REALITY IS THAT SOME GLASS BEADS ARE NOT ONLY MORE FASCINATING THAN SOME GEMSTONES BUT ALSO MORE EXPENSIVE. THE DELICATE SWIRL PATTERN AND PINK HUE OF THESE BOHEMIAN LAMPWORK GLASS BEADS CRY OUT TO BE ACCOMPANIED BY GOLD—OR AT LEAST VERMEIL AND GOLD-FILLED BEADS!

1. Start the bracelet by threading on a crimp. Pass the beading wire through the ring of one half of the clasp and back through the crimp. Make sure that the beading wire is tight around the ring and squeeze the crimp shut. Add a 3mm gold-filled round bead to cover the tail of the beading wire and cut.

2. Thread on three vermeil chips, a gold-filled round, a glass bead, and another gold-filled round. Repeat this pattern another seven times. Add three more chips and a gold-filled round.

3. Add the remaining crimp bead and bring the beading wire through the ring of the other side of the clasp and back through the crimp and last gf round bead. Tighten the bracelet so that all the beads fit snugly against each other. Close the crimp and snip off any remaining beading wire. Add the crimp covers.

4. To make the dangle, add a 3mm gold-filled bead to the head-pin, then a glass bead, another 3mm gold-filled bead, and 3 vermeil chips. Cut the headpin to leave about $5/8$" above the last bead. See Jewelry Techniques to make a wire-wrapped loop. Start the loop and slip it onto the beading wire between the crimp cover and the adjacent round bead. Close the loop and finish wrapping the wire around its base.

TOOLS
Crimping Pliers, Wire Cutters, Round-Nosed Pliers, Flat-Nosed Pliers

MATERIALS (7" BRACELET)
- 2 gold-filled crimp beads
- 1' of beading wire
- 1 vermeil hook-and-eye clasp
- 20 3mm gold-filled seamless hollow round beads
- 30 3mm to 4mm vermeil (or Thai silver) "chip" spacer beads
- 9 11mm Bohemian lampwork glass pink beads
- 2 gold-filled crimp covers
- 1 $1^{1}/_{2}$" vermeil headpin with ball tip

43.
CRYSTAL AND GOLD NECKLACE

THIS EXTRAVAGANT LOOKING NECKLACE RELIES MORE ON TIME AND EFFORT THAN THE VALUE OF THE MATERIALS. THE COLOR AND REFLECTIVITY OF THE HOLLOW GOLD-FILLED BEADS AND THE TINY BALL TIPS OF THE HEADPINS IS REDOUBLED BY THE LOVELY SWAROVSKI SIMPLICITY CRYSTALS. THE COLOR NAME OF THESE GLASS BEADS, "CRYSTAL GOLDEN SHADOW," IS WONDERFULLY DESCRIPTIVE. ALTHOUGH THE SPARKLING LITTLE CRYSTALS MIGHT PROVE ALL THAT GLITTERS IS NOT GOLD, THEY CERTAINLY MAGNIFY WHAT GOLD THERE IS.

1. Start the necklace by making the dangles. Add one crystal bead and one 2.5mm gold bead to a $1/2$" headpin. Make a simple loop. Repeat this until you have made all 189 dangles.

2. Pass the beading wire through the ring of one half of the clasp and back through the crimp. Make sure that the beading wire is tight around the ring and squeeze the crimp shut. Add a crystal bead and a 5mm gold round bead to cover the tail of the beading wire and cut.

3. Thread on a crystal bead and a 7mm gold bead. Repeat four times.

4. Add seven dangles, then a 7mm gold bead. Repeat this pattern twenty-six times or until the necklace is the length you wish. (Remember to try it around your neck to make sure.)

5. Add a crystal bead and a 7mm gold bead. Repeat three times. Add another crystal, a 5mm gold bead, and a crystal.

6. Bring the beading wire through the ring of the other side of the clasp and back through the crimp and round bead. Tighten the necklace so that there are no spaces between the beads, close the crimp, and snip off any remaining beading wire. Add the crimp covers.

TOOLS
Wire Cutters, Crimping Pliers, Round-Nosed Pliers

MATERIALS

201	4.5mm Swarovski 5310 (Simplicity) crystal Golden Shadow beads
189	2.5mm seamless hollow gold-filled round beads
189	$1/2$" gold-filled headpins with ball tip
20"	of beading wire
2	silver crimp beads
1	vermeil hook-and-eye clasp
36	7mm seamless hollow gold-filled round beads
2	5mm seamless hollow gold-filled round beads
2	2mm gold-filled crimp covers

44.
GOLD CHAIN AND ORGANIC BEADS

ALTHOUGH GOLD IS SELDOM USED WITH COMMON MATERIALS, AN EXCEPTION CAN BE MADE WITH SOME ORGANIC BEADS. BECAUSE THE COLOR OF GOLD BLENDS SO WELL WITH THEIR EARTHY TONES, THIS NECKLACE HAS THREE DIFFERENT PARTS. AS IN A CHARM NECKLACE, USE YOUR OWN SELECTION OF BEADS AND VARY THE PATTERN.

1. Start with the beading wire. Use a crimp bead to attach one end to a 6mm ring and arrange on it fourteen of the oblong shell beads and the 12mm shell bead, separated by 3 and 4mm round gold-filled beads and by three clusters of vermeil chip beads. (See photograph on page 108.) Using a crimp, attach the end of the beading wire to the other 6mm ring. Add the crimp covers.

2. Using the headpins, make three dangles, two with the abalone beads and a 2.5mm gold-filled round bead, and one with the remaining vermeil chips and two gold-filled round beads. Make a loop at the top of the dangle and attach each to the end ring of the beading wire strand using three of the 4mm jump rings.

3. Use the remaining beads and the gold-filled wire to make ten pendants with loops at each end. (I have used single beads for each pendant except for the two 14mm shell beads and the five horn discs.) Lay these pendants head to tail along with enough chain to make about 22" total. Now cut the chain into five pieces of different length and use them to link the ten pendants together, starting and ending with a pendant. If the pendants do not swivel freely on their wire, use a 4mm jump ring to attach them so there is more freedom of movement. Attach the ends of the pendant strand to the ends of the beading wire strand.

4. Take 18" of chain and attach each end to the link of chain immediately below the end pendants. The necklace is worn with the beading wire segment around the neck with the two chain strands falling in front.

TOOLS
Wire Cutters, Round-Nosed Pliers, Flat-Nosed Pliers

MATERIALS

20"	of gold-plated beading wire
2	gold-filled crimp beads
2	6mm gold-filled rings
15	25mm by 9mm (approximately) shell oblong beads
1	2mm pen shell bead
9	4mm gold-filled seamless hollow round beads
21	3mm gold-filled seamless hollow round beads
10	2.5mm gold-filled seamless hollow round beads
21	3mm to 6mm vermeil Thai silver chip beads
2	gold-filled crimp covers
3	1" gold-filled headpins with ball tip
2	10mm abalone beads
12	4mm gold-filled jump rings (heavy gauge)
2	large (40mm by 20mm to 30mm) shell oval beads
1	large (37mm by 35mm) bone carved turtle bead
2	2mm carved wood faceted beads
1	25mm bone carved round bead
1	18mm wood round bead
2	14mm shell beads shaped like grapefruit segments
5	3mm by 12mm horn disc beads
27"	of gold-filled chain with 15mm textured links and 7mm plain round links
20"	of 22 gauge gold-filled wire

45. SILVER "TUSK" NECKLACE

SHELL BEADS FROM THE NAGA TRIBES OF NORTHERN INDIA AND BURMA, ALONG WITH AN ORGANIC-LOOKING GEMSTONE SUCH AS JASPER, MATCHES THE TEXTURED, ALMOST ORGANIC FEEL OF THE SILVER "TUSK." JASPER COMES IN MANY VARIETIES OF PATTERN AND COLOR, SOME UNIQUE TO SPECIFIC MINES. THIS PARTICULAR ONE IS CALLED FIRE JASPER BECAUSE OF ITS GLOWING RED COLORATION. IF YOU CANNOT FIND THIS VARIETY, YOU COULD SUBSTITUTE OTHER JASPERS AND RETAIN THE SAME FEELING.

1. Thread the silk onto the beading needle. Double it and tie a double knot at the end. Put a dab of hypo-cement or nail polish on the knot and cut the tail very close to the knot. Thread on one half of the clasp so that the knot sits inside the ring. Tie another knot tightly against the outside of the clasp and then begin adding the beads.

2. Thread on two jasper beads (J), a larger (6mm) silver bead (LS), four J, one small (4mm) silver bead (SS), a turquoise nugget, SS, make a knot, J, LS, Naga shell bead, silver "tusk," 3mm red coral bead, Naga shell, SS, three J. Make a knot, LS, seven J, LS, J, SS, 6mm turquoise disc, SS, four J, LS, J. Make a knot.

3. Thread on the other half of the clasp. Make a knot and use your awl to get it tightly against the inside of the ring of the clasp. Make another knot on top of it and tighten it firmly. Add a dab of hypo-cement or clear nail polish and cut away the remaining thread.

THE HILL TRIBE PEOPLE OF BURMA AND NORTHERN THAILAND ARE FAMOUS FOR CREATING GREAT VARIETIES OF SILVER BEADS AND PENDANTS. THEIR SILVER IS MORE PURE THAN STERLING, RANGING FROM 950 TO 999 PARTS PER 1000. THIS MEANS THAT IT IS SOFTER AND EASIER TO WORK WITH SIMPLE TOOLS. A PATTERN IS FREQUENTLY INDENTED, AND THE NATURAL TAR-NISHING OF THE PITTED AREAS FORMS A PLEASING TEXTURE. MANY OF THE JEWELRY PIECES HAVE BEEN TREAS-URED BY FAMILIES OVER GENERA-TIONS, LEADING TO A WARM ANTIQUE GLOW.

TOOLS
Beading Needle, Awl, Hypo-Cement or Clear Nail Polish

MATERIALS

36"	of size F silk
1	silver hook-and-eye clasp
22	8mm "fire" jasper round beads (J)
5	6mm Thai silver disc beads (LS)
5	4mm Thai silver disc beads (SS)
1	35mm by 18mm (approximately) Chinese turquoise nugget bead
2	17mm Naga shell with inlaid turquoise round beads
1	100mm (approximately) Thai silver tusk-shaped bead
1	3mm red coral bead
1	6mm Chinese turquoise disc bead

NOTE
Hill tribe design styles are highly respected although often idiosyncratic. Here, I have used the spirit of hill tribe design to showcase an impressive Thai silver "tusk." Although you need a degree of courage to use large pieces like this in jewelry, the result can be very rewarding.

46.
"STARDUST" AND CHAIN EARRINGS

STARDUST IS THE NAME OF A CERTAIN TYPE OF SILVER FINISH. THE PLAIN SURFACE IS COATED WITH HUNDREDS OF TINY GRAINS OF SILVER THAT TWINKLE LIKE LITTLE STARS.

1. Cut the chain into two sections, each containing six rings. To one end of each attach two stardust balls by opening their loops. On the third ring, add another. On the fourth ring, add another. On the last ring, add one more.

2. Make the CZ dangles by adding one CZ bead to each of the headpins and making a simple loop. Attach one of these beside each single stardust ball, making sure to use three of each color in the same order on each earring.

3. Open the loops of the earwires and attach them to the fourth rings (from the two silver balls) of each piece of chain, making sure that you have used the same ring on each piece of the chain.

TOOLS
Flat-Nosed Pliers, Wire Cutters

MATERIALS
4" of silver chain with 10mm rings

10 4mm silver "stardust" balls with loops

6 4mm cubic zirconia (CZ) faceted round beads in three colors (two each in lime, pink, and purple)

6 $1/2$" silver headpins with ball tip

1 pair of silver earwires with green CZ

47.
SILVER CHAIN AND CRYSTAL EARRINGS

A FEW LINKS OF PRECIOUS METAL CHAIN CAN MAKE BEAUTIFUL EARRINGS, ESPECIALLY WHEN PAIRED WITH A SINGLE DRAMATIC BEAD. ADJUST THE NUMBER OF LINKS TO CREATE A LENGTH THAT FLATTERS YOUR NECK.

1. Cut the chain into two 2" sections. To one end of each attach the crystal bead using the 8mm jump ring.

2. To the other end attach the earwire by opening its loop and closing it around the last link of the chain.

TOOLS
Flat-Nosed Pliers, Wire Cutters

MATERIALS
4" of silver chain 15mm textured links joined by 7mm plain round links

2 22mm top-drilled Swarovski crystal aquamarine 6015 "polygon" beads

2 8mm silver jump rings

1 pair of silver earwires with blue cubic zirconia (CZ)

48.
GOLD FOIL LAMPWORK GLASS EARRINGS

A SIMPLER VARIATION OF THESE EARRINGS CAN BE CREATED REPLACING THE DANGLES WITH A SINGLE CRYSTAL BEAD ABOVE THE LAMPWORK BEAD.

1. To a headpin add a 3mm round bead, a daisy, a glass bead and another daisy and 3mm bead. Cut the headpin $5/8$" from the last bead and make a wire-wrapped loop (see Jewelry Techniques).

2. Add a crystal bead and a 2.5mm round bead to the stem of an earwire and make a simple half finished loop. Attach it to the wire-wrapped loop and close it to finish the earring.

TOOLS
Wire Cutters, Round Nose and Flat Nose Pliers

MATERIALS
- 2   20mm by 13mm Czech lampwork glass beads with gold foil.
- 2   4mm Swarovski crystal aurum bi-cone beads (5301)
- 4   4mm vermeil daisy spacer beads
- 2   2.5mm gold-filled hollow seamless round beads
- 4   3mm gold-filled hollow seamless round beads
- 2   2" gold-filled headpins with ball
- 2   gold-filled "add-on" earwires

49.
THAI SILVER AND HANDMADE GLASS EARRINGS

THE SILVER FOIL EMBEDDED IN THESE HANDMADE GLASS BEADS COUPLED WITH THE "BEAN" BEAD CREATES A THICK CENTRAL SILVER CORE FOR THE SOFT VIOLET HUES OF THE GLASS "WINGS."

1. Start the earring by adding a silver round bead to your headpin. Add a silver foil lamp bead, a "bean" bead, an d another round bead. Start making the beginning of a wire wrapped loop (see Jewelry Techniques).

2. Slip the loop onto the ring of the earwire and wrap the tail of the headpin around the base of the loop. Note: Make sure that "bean" bead sits so the decorated ends are perpendicular to the wings of the glass bead.

TOOLS
Wire Cutters, Round-Nosed Pliers, Flat-Nosed Pliers and Cutters

MATERIALS
- 2   10 by 15mm silver foil lamp beads
- 2   5 by 10mm Thai silver "bean" shape beads
- 4   2.5mm silver seamless hollow round beads
- 2   2 inch sterling silver head pins with a tri-dot decoration
- 1   pair sterling silver earwires

NOTE
Before starting this pair of earrings, you will need to read how to make a wire wrapped loop in the Techniques section.

50.
LAMPWORK GLASS AND CRYSTAL DANGLE EARRINGS

THESE LOVELY GLASS BEADS, WHICH USE TRADITIONAL EUROPEAN-STYLE GLASS TECHNIQUES TO CREATE CONTEMPORARY STYLE, ARE WRAPPED WITH GOLD FOIL. ALTHOUGH MOST SILVER AND GOLD FOIL BEADS ENCASE THE FOIL IN A LAYER OF GLASS, THIS GOLD SITS ON THE SURFACE AND APPEARS JUST AS RICH AS SOLID GOLD. BECAUSE IT IS PURE GOLD, IT WILL NOT TARNISH, AND BECAUSE IT IS FUSED TO THE MOLTEN GLASS DURING PRODUCTION, THE BOND IS PERMANENT. THE OUTSIDE GLASS SWIRL IS RAISED ABOVE THE LEVEL OF THE GOLD AND PROTECTS IT FROM ANY EXCESSIVE RUBBING.

1. To an eyepin, add a 2.5mm round bead, a daisy spacer bead, a glass bead, and another daisy spacer bead. Cut the eyepin $^5/_8$" from the last bead and begin a wire-wrapped loop (see Jewelry Techniques, page 129). Attach to the earwire and complete the wrapping of the loop.

2. To make the dangles, add a crystal bead and a 2mm round bead to a headpin. Make a simple half-finished loop. Attach it to a ring and finish closing the loop. Make and attach two more of these dangles to the ring.

3. Open the loop of the eyepin, attach the ring with the three dangles, and re-close the loop.

TOOLS
Wire Cutters, Round-Nosed Pliers, Flat-Nosed Pliers

MATERIALS
- 2 2" gold-filled eyepins
- 2 2.5mm gold-filled hollow seamless round beads
- 4 4mm vermeil daisy spacer beads
- 2 gold-filled earwires
- 2 20mm by 13mm Czech lampwork glass beads with gold foil
- 6 4mm Swarovski crystal aurum bi-cone beads (5301)
- 6 2mm gold-filled hollow seamless round beads
- 6 $^1/_2$" gold-filled headpins with ball tips
- 2 3.5mm gold-filled rings

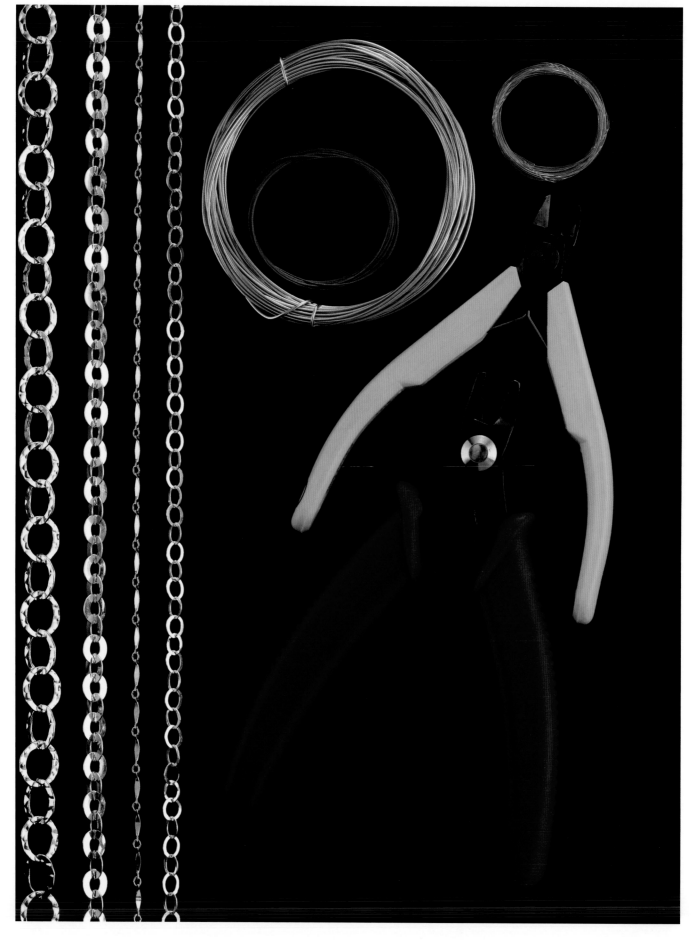

BASIC JEWELRY MAKING

During my many years as a jewelry maker, I've found that the following methods work well for me. More importantly, I have found that they work well for the people I have taught and for the thousands of people who have been taught by our Beadworks' instructors.

Some of these techniques are simple and require hardly any practice, although dexterity is a big help. Others need patience and several attempts to get them right. If you find yourself becoming frustrated, remember that it is mostly a matter of familiarity. If at first you don't succeed, cut the beads off the thread or wire and start all over again!

There are also many bead stores and educational organizations that offer beading classes. If you are the sort of person who learns best through hands-on teaching, they provide a quick way to get started.

To begin working with beads, you need a well-lit, flat, hard surface with some kind of soft covering to stop the beads from rolling around. If you are going to work at a table or desk, you can buy bead mats or bead design boards or simply use a towel. Personally, I prefer to work on my studio floor, which is well carpeted and allows me to surround myself with tools and beads and a cat to keep me company. Have a mirror nearby so that you can check the look and length of your necklaces and earrings.

Good tools make everything a lot easier. I always use two pairs of flat-nosed pliers, one of them with very narrow jaws. Your round-nosed pliers should have tips narrow enough to make really small loops. If you discover a love for making jewelry, treat yourself to a really good quality pair of wire cutters.

Once you are seriously into making jewelry, lots of little containers are essential for storing your beads and findings. These can be anything from old jars to specialized bead vials, but it does help if they are transparent and have lids. Multi-compartment plastic boxes are also a great storage method.

But don't worry about accumulating lots of tools and gadgets at the beginning. Pick one of the easier designs and just get started!

THE GOLDEN RULES

The carpenter's maxim is "measure twice, cut once." The wise jewelry maker measures a necklace and bracelet at least twice, and then tries it around the neck or wrist for size. She lays it down and double checks the pattern. Only then does she make the final knot or squeeze the last crimp bead shut. Never finish off your jewelry until you are absolutely sure it is right!

Don't let a little clumsy work spoil the whole piece. If you forgive a bad knot or a missed spacer, you will see the flaw every time you wear the jewelry. Better to start over and get it right.

Don't ruin good ingredients by mixing in poor ones. Even if the material is hidden by the beads or under your hair at the back of your neck, use good quality. (Never, ever, string anything on fishing line!)

Assume you are going to make mistakes. I constantly make mistakes, even after many, many years of jewelry making! If the recipe calls for two headpins, understand that you will need at least two more on standby in case you cut them too short or bend them too badly. If it requires twenty inches of beading wire, make sure you have the rest of the spool nearby in case you need to start all over again.

Don't waste time looking for the exact bead called for in a recipe. Use a substitute of the same quality with similar design values (color, size, shape, texture).

Never pass up a good bead. If you see one you really, really love, buy it and let it inspire a future design.

I.
USING CRIMP BEADS TO ATTACH CLASPS

Crimps are little hollow tubes that can be crushed together to grip strands of beading wire. You use them like this.

1. Pass the beading wire through the crimp, then through the loop of the clasp and back through the crimp again. With a pair of crimping pliers or flat-nosed pliers, squeeze the crimp until it firmly grips both strands of the wire (llus. A and B).

2. Snip off the tail of the wire as close to the crimp as possible (llus. C).

A slightly more sophisticated finish can be achieved by using crimp covers. These fit over the flattened crimp and are gently squeezed shut to create the look of a normal bead. However, you can only use crimp covers if you have previously used crimping pliers to flatten the crimp.

Another trick is to hide the tail of the beading wire inside an adjacent bead(s). I always do this if the hole in those beads is big enough to hold two thicknesses of beading wire, and I often add a spacer bead to the end of my design just to permit this method to be used.

1. Pass the beading wire through one or more beads, then through the crimp and through the loop of the clasp.

2. As you bring the beading wire back through the crimp, push it further back through the bead(s).

3. Squeeze the crimp shut, and snip the tail of the wire as close as possible to the last bead it was passed through. This way, the tail end of the beading wire will recoil very slightly and be hidden inside the last bead.

A

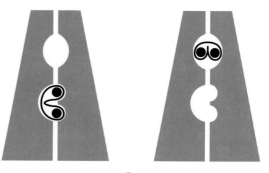

B

C

II.
USING JUMP RINGS
AND SPLIT RINGS

HOW TO USE JUMP RINGS

1. With a pair of flat-nosed pliers, grip the jump ring so that it lies flat between the pliers with the join slightly to one side of them.

2. Grip the other side of the join with your fingers. Twist the ring sideways so that it opens.

3. After looping the ring through the piece or pieces you are connecting, close it by once again gripping it with the pliers and twisting the wire back until the two ends meet and the join is closed. Make sure that the two ends of the wire are flush with each other.

Never open jump rings by pulling the ends apart, as they will be much more difficult to close. Always twist them sideways as described above.

HOW TO USE SPLIT RINGS

1. Although you can buy a specialty tool to open these, the simplest way is just to slip your fingernail between the split parts of the ring just behind the opening. This should create just enough space to let you push the piece you wish to connect into the split of the ring.

2. Rotate the ring until the connected item has traveled all the way along the split and out of the opposite side. You may want to use your flat-nosed pliers to help rotate the ring.

III.
GETTING KNOTTED: THE ART OF USING SILK THREAD

Strands of beads are sometimes strung on silk thread, which is thought to offer the best compromise between strength and flexibility. It is best to thread the beads onto a doubled strand of silk, both to add strength and to increase the size of the knots. While you can use silk thread without knotting between each bead, it is traditional to make these knots in order to highlight each bead and to prevent them from chafing against each other.

STRINGING ON SILK THREAD

You need a needle to draw the thread through the beads. While any thin needle will do, flexible twisted wire needles make the job a lot easier.

1. Thread the silk through the eye of the needle and draw it through until the doubled length is enough for the necklace (Illus. A). If you are knotting between each bead, your doubled strand should be at least twice as long as the finished necklace. For example, an 18" knotted necklace will require 2 yards, or 72", of silk thread. If you are not knotting between each bead, the doubled thread should be about 6" longer than the finished piece. An 18" necklace will therefore require 4 feet, or 48", of thread.

2. Tie the doubled end of the thread with a simple overhand knot (Illus. B). Pull on the tail with your pliers to tighten the knot.

3. To tighten the knot even more, separate the two threads and pull apart (Illus. C).

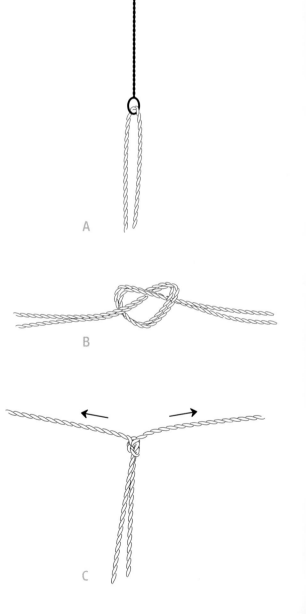

A

B

C

USING AN AWL TO MAKE KNOTS

An awl is a metal needle with a long handle that is used for getting knots to sit snugly against beads or bead tips. It is very simple to use once you know how. You can use the next step to practice knotting. Once you begin to make a real necklace, you will first have to attach the clasp (see page 124).

1. Add a bead to the thread. Make an overhand knot anywhere along the thread, but do not tighten it. Put the point of the awl through the knot, and gently reduce the size of the knot until it fits loosely around the awl (Illus. A). Put your finger on the thread so that the knot lies between your finger and the awl.

2. Keeping your finger on the knot, move the awl toward the bead. You should be able to easily move the knot all the way down the thread until it lies snugly against the bead (Illus. A).

3. Once you have the knot in position, slowly remove the awl as you pull on the thread to tighten the knot (Illus. B).

4. To tighten the knot even more, you can separate the two threads and pull them apart to help force the knot closer to the bead (Illus. C).

5. Add another bead and push it firmly against the knot you have just made. Make another knot as described in steps 1–3. Make sure the beads lie snugly against one another. Continue practicing with a few beads until you are confident that you have the technique mastered.

TOOLS TIPS

When you need to knot and can't find your awl, fold out a safety pin and use that.

If you've lost your scissors or can't find your cutters, get out your nail clippers. They are usually very sharp and you can get them nice and close to your bead to cut off excess thread or wire.

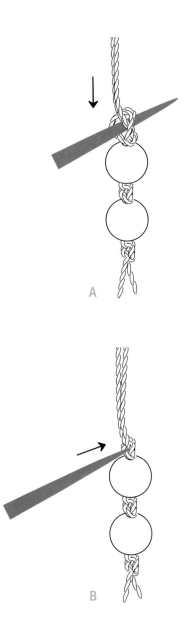

A

B

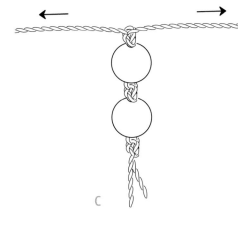

C

IV.
USING BEAD TIPS
TO ATTACH CLASPS

When stringing on silk thread (see "Getting Knotted" on page 122,) you need to finish off the ends in a way that will let you attach them to the two halves of a clasp. The little findings that enable you to do this are called bead tips. One end of a bead tip is a simple loop that will connect to the clasp. The other end grips the knot at the end of your thread.

To use either kind of bead tip, start with your thread doubled and knotted at the end.

TO USE STRING-THROUGH CLAMSHELL BEAD TIPS

1. Make another overhand knot on top of the first knot at the end of your doubled thread. This is easier to do if you use your awl to guide the loop of the second knot so it sits on the first. Tighten that knot as well. Unless you are very sure of your knots, add a dab of hypo-cement (a clear glue with a precision applicator) or clear nail polish. Trim off the excess tail of the thread with a pair of sharp scissors (Illus. A, B, C, D).

2. Pass your needle and thread into the open clamshell of the bead tip and through the hole at the base of the shell. Pull the thread completely through so that the knot sits snugly inside the clamshell. Using flat-nosed pliers, gently squeeze the sides of the shell together so that it closes around the knot and grips it firmly (Illus. E, F).

3. Make another single knot tight against the bottom of the bead tip. Now add the beads to the length of the silk thread to create your necklace.

4. Once you have finished stringing all the beads of your necklace, finish it off by passing the needle and thread through the hole on the outside of another bead tip. (Remember to make a knot after the last bead.)

5. Pull the thread so that the last knot of your necklace sits firmly against the outside of the bead tip. Now tie an overhand knot so that it sits inside the clamshell of the bead tip. To position the knot properly, use your awl to move the loop of the knot as close to the inside wall of the bead tip as possible. Tighten the knot, pulling the awl out at the last moment.

6. Make a second overhand knot, and tighten it on top of the first. Add a dab of hypo-cement if needed. Using flat-nosed pliers, gently squeeze the sides of the shell together so that it closes around the knot and grips it firmly. Using a sharp pair of scissors, trim off the rest of the thread as close to the outside of the bead tip as possible.

7. You now have a strand with a bead tip at either end. Put the open loop of one bead tip through the ring on one half of the clasp. Use flat-nosed pliers to close the loop so that it is firmly attached to the ring. Attach the other bead tip to the other part of the clasp in the same manner.

TIP

If you add a few smaller beads to the beginning and end of your necklace, it will be easier to open and undo the clasp when you wear it.

QUICK TRICK

If you have an idea for a necklace but don't have the time to make it up, string a few beads defining at least part of the design on a piece of thread or even fishing line and tie off both ends. This way, you will be able to remember what the idea was when you find time to make it.

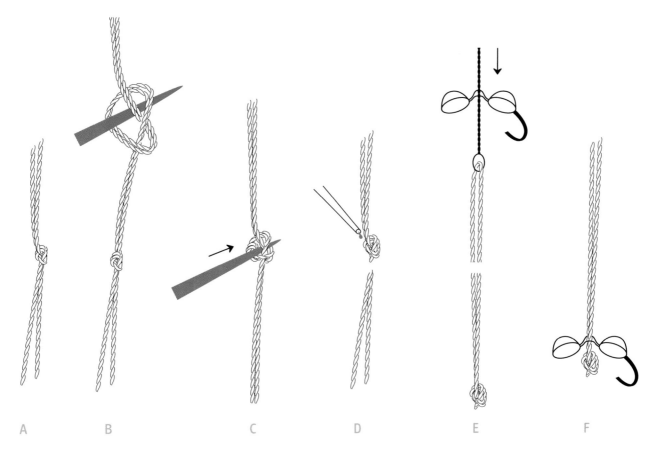

A   B   C   D   E   F

USING BASKET BEAD TIPS

While it is a little more difficult to make the final knot using this style of bead tip, basket beads give a more sophisticated look to your jewelry—if you can master the technique.

1. Take the end of the doubled thread and tie a simple overhand knot. Tighten it by gripping the tail with pliers and pulling. Trim off the excess tail of the thread with a pair of sharp scissors (Illus. A).

2   Pass your needle and thread into the basket and through the hole at its bottom. Pull the thread completely through so that the knot sits snugly inside the bottom of the basket. Put a tiny dab of hypo-cement or clear nail polish on the knot (Illus. B, C, D).

3. Make another overhand knot near the outside of the bead tip, and use your awl to move the loop of that knot tight against the bottom of the basket. This knot keeps the beads from chafing against the bead tip and improve the overall appearance.

4. Now add the beads to the silk thread to create your necklace (Illus. E).

A   B   C   D   E

5. Once you have completed stringing all the beads of your
    necklace, make an overhand knot, and use the awl to position
    it tightly against the last bead. Pass the needle and thread
    through the hole on the outside bottom of another basket
    bead tip. Pull the thread until the bead tip sits firmly against
    the knot after the last bead (Illus. F).

6. Tie an overhand knot, and use your awl to move the loop of
    the knot as close as possible to the bottom inside wall of the
    bead tip (Illus. G). Tighten the knot, pulling the awl out at the
    last moment. It takes a little practice to get this final knot to slip
    into the basket, but it is important to get a good tight fit so that
    no thread can be seen once the necklace is complete. Add a tiny
    dab of hypo-cement or clear nail polish to firmly secure this
    knot (Illus. H).

7. Finish off by attaching the ends of the bead tips to the clasp as
    above (Illus. I, J).

F   G   H   I   J

V.
USING HEADPINS AND EYEPINS

Headpins and eyepins are convenient ways of attaching beads to necklaces, earwires, and other findings. Simply add some beads and make a loop at the top in the following manner:

1. Hold the bottom of the pin to make sure the beads are sitting tightly against it, and cut the top of the pin to the correct length for the loop. For a 3mm loop, there should be a $1/4$" of pin above the last bead. Small loops are made by gripping the wire toward the tips of the plier jaws. Grip the wire further back to create a larger loop, being sure to allow more wire between the bead and the end of the pin. When you practice this technique, it is useful to make a mark on the jaws of your round-nosed pliers so that you know where to place the wire between the jaws (llus. A).

2. Grip the top of the pin between the jaws of your round-nosed pliers. Make a "P" shape by rolling the pliers away from you. Move the pliers around if necessary until the tip of the pin meets the wire at the top of the bead (llus. B).

3. Put your fingernail behind the neck of the "P," where it touches the bead, and bend the loop back until it is centered above the bead. Your finished loop should look like a balloon with the string hanging straight down (llus. C).

4. To attach the loop to another loop or ring, open it to the side as with the jump ring below.

NOTE

If you are wire-wrapping on a headpin or eyepin, follow the instructions on page 127, substituting the headpin or eyepin for the wire. For larger loops, allow more distance on the wire. Remember, the wire's placement on the jaws of your pliers determines the size of your loop.

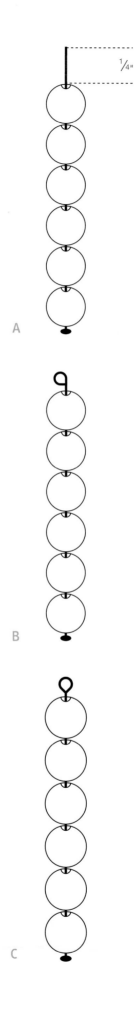

A

B

C

VI.
WIRE WRAPPING

This technique can be used with precious metal and other wires or with headpins and eyepins. It forms a stronger loop and adds a space between the loop and the bead. You will need to practice this technique many times to master it. Create a small wire-wrapped loop at each end of a bead in the following manner:

1. Cut a piece of wire to the width of your bead plus about $1^1/2$" (Illus. A).

2. With round-nosed pliers, grip the wire about $1/2$" from the end. Bend the wire around the pliers until a loop is formed and the tail of the wire is perpendicular to the stem (Illus. B).

3. With your fingernail behind the loop, use the round-nosed pliers to roll it back until it is centered above the stem of the wire (Illus. C).

4. Using your finger or fingernail, wrap the tail of the wire around the stem a couple of turns. Use flat-nosed pliers to finish wrapping the tail tightly. Snip off any excess wire (Illus. D, E).

5. Place a bead on the wire. Grip the wire so that the jaws are about $3/8$" from the bead, and roll the pliers until a loop is formed and the tail of the wire is perpendicular to the stem (Illus. F, B).

6. With your fingernail behind the loop, roll it back until it is centered above the stem of the wire (Illus. C).

7. Using your finger or fingernail, wrap the tail of the wire around the stem a couple of turns, getting it tight between the bead and the loop. Use flat-nosed pliers to finish wrapping the tail tightly. Snip off any excess wire (Illus. D, E).

NOTE
When making a single loop on a headpin or eyepin, cut the wire about $5/8$" above the bead when making a medium size loop.

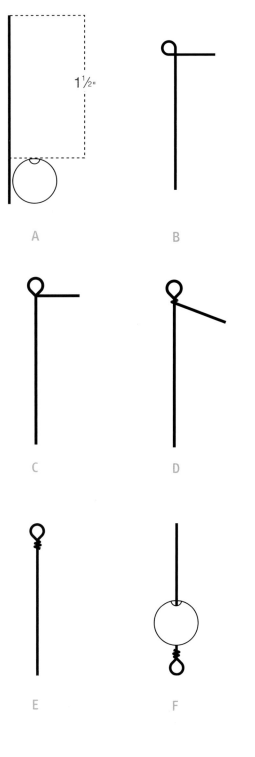

A   B

C   D

E   F

STANDARD MEASUREMENTS

SIZE

The diameter of beads is commonly described in millimeters. The chart at right shows the most common sizes, from 2 to 12 millimeters.

Since beads are often sold in strands measured by the inch, it is useful to know how many beads there are per inch. It is especially useful to know how many comprise a 16-inch strand, a typical length for temporarily strung beads.

LENGTH

One inch = 25.4 millimeters
One foot = 0.3 meters
One millimeter = .04 inches
One meter = 3.3 feet

THICKNESS

Wire thicknesses are measured in American standard gauge or inches or millimeters. The higher the gauge number, the thinner the wire.

Beading wire thicknesses are measured in inches. Note that the last three gauges in the chart to the right are roughly equivalent to the beading wire sizes of .018, .015, and .013.

WHEN IS AN OUNCE NOT AN OUNCE

When we refer to an ounce of silver and gold, we do not mean the ounce that you use to measure flour on your kitchen scale. Normal, everyday weights are calculated in "avoirdupois" ounces. But silver and gold are special and have a weight all their own: the "Troy" ounce. Named after the French city of Troyes where it was a weight at a popular medieval trading fair, it is about 10 percent heavier than its avoirdupois (French again, from " have weight") cousin. A Troy ounce is about 31 grams versus the less substantial 28 grams of an ordinary ounce.

APPROXIMATE BEADS PER INCH

		1"	7"	16"	18"
Bead Size	2 mm	12	88	200	225
	3 mm	8	59	134	150
	4 mm	6	44	100	114
	5 mm	5	35	80	90
	6 mm	4	29	67	76
	7 mm	3.5	25	58	65
	8 mm	3	22	50	57
	9 mm	2.5	19	45	40
	10 mm	2.5	17	40	45
	12 mm	2	14	33	38

WEIGHT CONVERSIONS

1 grain = .0648 grams

1 carat = 0.2 grams

1 gram = 5 carats = .03527 ounces = 15.43 grains

1 avoirdupois ounce = 28.35 grams = 437.5 grains

1 troy ounce = 31.1 grams = 480 grains = 1.097 avoirdupois ounces

WIRE THICKNESS

18-gauge = .0403 inches = 1.02 mm
20-gauge = .0320 inches = 0.81 mm
22-gauge = .0253 inches = 0.64 mm
24-gauge = .0201 inches = 0.51 mm
26-gauge = .0159 inches = 0.40 mm
28-gauge = .0126 inches = 0.32 mm

NECKLACE LENGTHS

One of the pleasures of creating your own jewelry is that you can adjust the length of your necklaces so they fit you. A comfortable choker on some necks is a genuine strangler on others, and a centerpiece that is well presented on the faint décolletage of a fashion model might be entirely lost on those who are more generously endowed. If the jewelry is for yourself, disregard the standard lengths and try it on for size as you are making it.

Unless otherwise stated, the necklace ingredients and instructions in this book are for 16-inch necklaces, the so-called "standard" short length. If this length does not suit you, adjust it by adding or subtracting from the ingredients and adjusting the pattern accordingly.

GETTING THE LENGTH RIGHT

Although you can lay out all your beads in a line and measure them, or place them in the channels of a marked beading board, there is really only one sure way of getting the length right. Just before you think you are halfway through stringing the beads, hold the uncompleted necklace with the clasp at the back of your neck. Looking in a mirror, you can then judge exactly where the strand will fall. This step is critical in any necklace with a centerpiece or a centered pattern, but it is something I do with every single necklace I am making for myself.

THE "STANDARDS"

Although you will decide the right lengths for your own body, it is useful for jewelry makers to have a general reference guide. There are a variety of opinions about terminology and standard lengths. One woman's "long opera" is another's "rope." The following is as good a guide as any, but remember that the best standard lengths are those you create for yourself. Since a bracelet is, to the maker, just a very short necklace, we start with that length.

Bracelet	7 to 8 inches
Choker	13 to 15 inches
Standard short	16 to 17 inches
Standard long	18 to 20 inches
Matinee	About 24 inches
Opera	30 to 40 inches
Rope	40 inches and over

LENGTH

A 16-inch strand of beads, knotted with a fish hook clasp will be about 18 inches long when it's finished.

If 18 inches isn't long enough, add a few sterling or gold-filled round beads before the clasp. Or if you are using a hook clasp, add some chain to your bead tip on the opposite side to the hook.

BUYING SILVER AND GOLD

Buying silver beads is fairly straightforward. If there is a reputable bead store near you, they should carry a selection of silver beads, either individually or on temporary strands. That selection should include seamless hollow rounds in several sizes, other spacer beads, and individual silver beads of character. All silver should be of sterling fineness (925) or higher. Silver beads are also widely available by mail order or online.

Gold beads can take a little more effort to acquire. A good bead store might carry a range of vermeil and gold-filled beads. When you are buying vermeil, you should select it for the color of the gold coating. Personally, I prefer vermeil to look like at least 18 karat gold. If you are going to buy a bead that is essentially colored silver, you may as well choose the color of gold you like best. When gold-platers describe vermeil as a specific karat, they are usually talking about the color they are trying to match rather than the precise gold content. Of course, the thickness of the plating is important, but unless you have access to an X-ray machine, you will not be able to tell. A decent plating should be expected to last a long time on beads that are not rubbed against other surfaces.

Buying real gold beads can require a little more searching and I list a few contacts in the resources section of the book. Gold bead and finding prices fluctuate with the price for gold as a commodity. In times when the gold price is rapidly changing, the price of gold jewelry components will follow the market. During periods when gold becomes more expensive, you can at least console yourself with the thought that any gold you already own has gone up in value. Your first question about any gold item should be regarding its purity or karat value. Despite their popularity in Asia, I find 24 and 22 karat golds too soft for jewelry. A respectable and very popular fineness in the United States is 14 karat, but since it is more than 40 percent some other metal, it can tarnish or react with sensitive skins. Personally, I prefer the more international standard of 18 karats—it is strong enough to maintain its appearance and, with 75 percent gold content, will not tarnish or affect the skin under normal wear. But this decision is simply a matter of taste and budget.

DEFINING GOLD-FILLED

To be called gold-filled (G.F.), an object must contain 10 karat (or better) gold, comprising at least one-twentieth of its gross weight. If the amount of gold used in this method is less than one-twentieth of the weight of the bead, then it is called rolled-gold. When buying gold-filled beads, 14 karat is a good fineness. The designation: $1/20$ 14K G.F indicates that at least one-twentieth of the weight of the item is 14 karat gold.

FAKING GOLD

The ancient alchemists never succeeded in their quest to turn base metals into gold, but several methods have been devised to make them look like gold.

GOLD PLATE

The most commonly used modern method is electrolytic plating, during which a very thin layer of gold is deposited on a base metal bead. To imagine how thin this layer is you must realize that it is measured by millionths of an inch and is hundreds of times thinner than a human hair. Beads and findings made by this process can look attractive initially, but the normal wear of jewelry can rub away patches of the plating wherever it comes in contact with another object. I do not use gold-plated base metal in any of these projects because the objects possess little real value and are not suitable to use in fine jewelry.

GOLD-FILLED

Although gold-plated base metal is seldom an attractive material for fine jewelry, gold-filled often provides an inexpensive but respected alternative to real gold. In this method, the gold is fused or "sweated" on to the base metal by using heat and pressure. The bond is durable and because the layer is up to 200 times thicker than electroplating, the gold does not wear away under normal use.

VERMEIL

Fortunately, there is a much happier way to achieve the look and feel of gold jewelry at a modest cost. Although gold plating simply produces a gold-colored base metal, gold plating silver makes an admirable material called vermeil.

Nowadays, vermeil is produced through the same electrolytic method as gold plate. The official standard for designating an object vermeil is a layer of gold a hundred millionths of an inch thick over sterling silver. I suspect, however, that in the case of beads and findings, it is a thickness standard more honored in the breach than the observance. The great majority of vermeil beads are overlaid with a much thinner coating, although it is frequently of higher karat value than the minimum standard. In general, the term is used to indicate that the plating is real gold on real silver and you should expect that a bead referred to as vermeil is silver of at least sterling fineness and that it is coated in gold of at least 14 karats. Because the actual thickness of the plating can only be determined by an X-ray of the object, you should simply be aware that the plating, sooner or later, wears away.

For those who make their own jewelry, vermeil has another attraction: If the gold wears off, you can simply send the beads to an electro-plater and have them re-plated. So, except in the case of wire and some findings in which gold-filled is a better choice, use good-quality vermeil when you do not have the inclination or the budget to use solid gold.

STRETCHING IT OUT

There is a strong case for making a little gold or silver go a long way—both because they are expensive and because, well, you can! Good design ruthlessly exploits the metals' malleability to stretch them to the limit. Silver and gold are not just soft but have an extraordinary plastic quality that enables them to be beaten, pressed, and pulled into the thinnest of sheets or wires. With fine craftsmanship and creative thought these can be turned into an endless array of jewelry components.

FOIL (LEAF)

Gold and silver leaf or foil are at the extreme end of economy. With little effort, both metals can be pounded into leaves so thin and light that they will float like feathers on the air. A standard piece of silver or gold foil is as thin as one ten-thousandth of a millimeter, just a fraction of the thickness of a human hair.

This foil has been used for centuries to make base metal objects look like gold or silver. First a thin layer of varnish is applied to the metal. Then, using a fine brush and static electricity gathered by rubbing it on hair or fur, the leaf is picked up and laid onto the surface of the metal in a technique known as cold gilding.

But although foil is still sometimes used by jewelers to produce items like brooches or pendants, it is not practical for the surface of beads. The layer of gold or silver is simply so thin that it will be worn away as parts of a necklace rub against each other or against the skin. It is, however, a wonderful material for transforming glass beads into

SWEET GOLD

For centuries it has been popular in India to decorate sweets and desserts with silver and gold. Hammered into gossamer-thin sheets called varak, the precious metals become so insubstantial that a mere breath would destroy them if they were not adhered to the surface of a sticky confection. Tasteless, odorless, and inert, they pass through the human body with no effect, their only purpose being to add a touch of glamorous extravagance to the dish.

exquisite little jewels. Lampwork or flame-worked glass beads are individually made by melting the tip of a glass rod over a flame or torch. The molten glass is gathered on a metal rod, then turned and molded into the required shape. Using different colored glass, the artisan can create beads of great complexity in a dazzling range of hues. Going one stage further, the highly skilled worker can also encase a piece of gold or silver foil between the layers of glass, adding a marvelous reflectivity and richness to the bead. Because the fragile leaf is encased in glass, it is protected from wear and, in the case of silver, from tarnishing. These glass foil creations are often among the most beautiful beads in the world and deserve a prominent place in the design lexicon of silver and gold jewelry.

SHEETS AND WIRES

Although leaf is too insubstantial to do anything except coat another material, thin sheets of gold and silver can be used to create beads and pendants. Cut into small pieces, they are shaped, bent, and fused to each other to build up larger objects that give an impression of size and substance. Just as a house is constructed from thin ribs and sheets of wood, so beads can be created from these building blocks of silver and gold. Wires are used not only for connecting beads but to make the beads themselves. They are sometimes used independently to make light, basket-like beads but more often fused to the surface of sheets to create endless varieties of patterns.

HOLLOWNESS

Where gold and silver are concerned a hollow character can be a definite advantage. An ancient method of forming thin sheets of gold around a resin base is still used to create charming round beads that completely fool the eye and seem like solid gold until you pick them up and experience their extreme lightness.

Modern technology has also created a wide range of completely hollow gold and silver beads. The best of these are seamless and indistinguishable to the eye from solid metal. Indeed, it is almost pointless to buy plain round solid gold or silver beads when you can buy hollow beads for a small fraction of the price.

It is not just round beads that are hollow, however. Thousands of styles of silver and gold beads use the attribute of hollowness to reduce their weight and thus their cost. Many of the designs in these pages use hollow beads to make the jewelry affordable without losing any of its effect.

WORTH YOUR WEIGHT IN GOLD

Gold is very, very heavy. Imagine a cube just fifteen inches high, fifteen inches deep, and fifteen inches wide. Sitting on your (strongly reinforced) dining table, it would occupy little more than the space required for a place setting. Yet, if it were made of solid 24 karat gold, it would weigh one ton, almost as much as a small car.

CARING FOR SILVER AND GOLD

SILVER

Admirable as it is in all other respects, silver has one small failing—it tarnishes. This is not common, everyday oxidation, like the rust on iron or the patina on copper, but a reaction with hydrogen sulfide that dulls its surface with a coating of silver sulfide.

Unfortunately, hydrogen sulfide is not uncommon in today's industrial air environments, and even lurks in the kitchen, emanating from innocent-looking onions and eggs. Keep silver away from items containing sulfur, particularly rubber, which will quickly form a nasty mark. Chlorine, bromine, and ozone also lead to silver tarnish, so both salty and polluted airs are quick to cause discoloring. Even if one avoids all of these, sterling silver has a small percentage of copper that oxidizes in ordinary clean air. After prolonged exposure to any air, most sterling silver begins to lose its bright gleam.

Often, the tarnish is just a slight patina that gives the silver a pleasant warmth, but if it becomes dull or black, it's time to recapture the sparkle. Fortunately simple polishing with a soft cloth removes light layers of tarnish, and heavier deposits can be quickly defeated using a commercial silver dip such as Goddard's. Be careful not to leave items in the dip longer than instructed. In general, thirty seconds in the dip, a rinse under fresh water, and a quick buff dry takes care of most jobs. Do not put gemstones into silver dip. When cleaning jewelry with a mixture of silver and gemstones, try to buff just the silver areas with a soft cloth or an anti-tarnish jewelry cloth.

Here's a clever way to clean silver using tin foil and a little baking soda, which relies on the fact that the metal aluminum is even more attracted to sulfur:

a) Line a pan with aluminum foil. Lay your silver items on the aluminum foil.

b) Boil enough water to cover the items in the pan. Add a dash of salt and a tablespoon or two of baking soda. (You can experiment with different proportions.)

c) While still very hot, pour this mixture over the silver and watch the tarnish slowly disappear. (The silver must be in contact with the aluminum foil for this to work.) When the tarnish is gone, rinse the items with fresh water and buff them dry with a soft cloth.

"GOOD" TARNISH

Remember that tarnish on some silver beads is to be appreciated rather than removed. Do not clean away all the black from antiqued beads, and think carefully before cleaning any silver beads that are genuine antiques—part of their appeal and much of their value might be in the patina you are about to destroy. Gold can be cleaned by rinsing it under warm water with a little liquid detergent, if necessary. To remove tarnish from low karat gold, use a little all-metal cleaner then rinse it under warm water before buffing dry.

I am told the method works because the aluminum takes the sulfur from the tarnish (silver sulfide) and leaves just the silver behind. The tarnish, in effect, turns back into silver. Some people like this method because they feel it does not actually remove any silver, which is the case in polishing or using a silver dip. But metallurgists point out that the bond holding this converted silver to the surface is fairly weak, and that it is probably lost when it is buffed dry.

However you clean the tarnish from your silver, you remove such a miniscule amount of the actual metal that solid silver objects will last for many generations. Silver plate should be treated much more carefully, as the thin layer of silver can be worn away by aggressive polishing.

To avoid tarnish, store your silver in a dry place wrapped in a soft cloth or acid-free tissue paper inside a zip-lock bag. If you expel the air from the bag and close it firmly, the silver should remain completely untarnished indefinitely. In practice, I usually forget about the cloth or paper and just put each individual piece in an airtight bag, which protects them from tarnishing and rubbing against other pieces of jewelry.

There are also patented formulas that protect against tarnish, like Tarni-Shield and a remarkable product originally developed at the British Museum called Renaissance Wax.

GOLD

Solid gold does not require any special protection when it is worn, except from scratching (and perhaps theft). It is wise, however, to remember that items made from vermeil or gold plate rely on the effect of a very thin layer of gold and should be kept away from situations in which the surface could be damaged by scratching or rubbing.

Some people are surprised when their gold shows signs of discoloration or tarnish. It is true that pure gold does not corrode, but the copper or silver that is mixed with lower karat gold is susceptible to chemicals in air, perspiration, and cosmetics. Thus, lower karat gold is far more likely to show signs of tarnishing than higher karat. More than 40 percent of 14 karat gold is some other metal, so it really isn't surprising that tarnishing occurs. If you find that low karat gold discolors on your skin, try wearing 18 karat or higher, which should solve the problem.

STORING GOLD JEWELRY

Whether gold or vermeil, it is best to keep necklaces in a soft jewelry roll with a layer of cloth between any other pieces of jewelry that might harm their surfaces. If you keep them in a box, avoid jumbling them up with other jewelry. The sharp surface of gemstones can scratch even solid gold.

RESOURCES

The materials used in this book are available at fine beading stores everywhere. You can find many of them at Beadworks stores and at www.beadworks.com.

There are several internet directories of bead stores including:
www.beadshopfinder.com
Look for bead stores by city or by name.
www.guidetobeadwork.com
Worldwide index to wholesale suppliers, as well as retail stores.
www.mapmuse.com
Go to "crafts," then to "beading shops" to quickly find a bead store location near you.

For information on Swarovski Crystal products: www.create-your-style.com. Ask your local bead supplier for recommendations for crystal projects, too.

A number of publications serve the bead customer and have large resource listings. Some of my favorites include:
Lapidary Journal www.lapidaryjournal.com
Go to "find supplies."
Beadwork Magazine
www.interweave.com/bead/beadwork_magazine
Click on "resources" then go to "shopping."

If you are interested in learning more about the story of these fascinating metals, the following websites contain general information and links:
The Silver Institute   www.silverinstitue.org
World Gold Council   www.gold.org

If you are inspired by the designs in this book but too busy to make them yourself, visit www.NancyAlden.com for a range of made-up silver and gold jewelry.

NOTE

Due to the growing popularity of beading, there is now a wide selection of places to buy beads, findings, and threading materials. In North America alone there are more than a thousand bead stores as well as dozens of Internet retailers.

However, while shopping online can be quick and convenient, nothing beats the experience of visiting a well-stocked bead store. There, you are able to feel the texture of the beads and arrange them side-by-side to see if the combinations please you. If you cannot find exactly the bead you are looking for, you can ask your local supplier to help you find a suitable substitution. Adding your own creative flair will give you a piece of jewelry that is uniquely yours.

Keep in mind, though, that bead stores open (and close) at a rapid pace, so it is best to use the Internet or a phone directory to find them, then call to ask what kind of a selection they have. Most stores have at least a basic range of silver and perhaps some vermeil. Many, however, do not carry solid gold beads and findings, although they may be able to order them for you. Before driving miles with a vision of a golden necklace in your mind, check to see that they have the type of beads you need.

ACKNOWLEDGMENTS

The jewelry in this book was designed and created by Nancy Alden.

Susan Moffat made the PMC beads for the Kyanite and Precious Metal Clay necklace.

I would like to thank my editor, Shawna Mullen, who conceived and nurtured this project, and my fellow bead supplier, Irene Chen, whose dynamic business skills helped to introduce thousands of new beads into the hands of contemporary designers.

Thanks also to the following people for their work on the book:

William Brinson, photography
Mai Tran, styling
Lola Neasse, styling assistance
Denise Cermanski, photo assistance
Jennifer Wechsler, jewelry design assistance
Liz Doughty and Ivannia Gomez, jewelry components coordination
Stephen Sammons, research
Everyone at Potter Craft including Lauren Monchik, Rosy Ngo,
Isa Loundon, Christina Schoen, Mona Michael, Amy Sly, and
Alison Forner

Most especially, I thank all of my colleagues and customers whose great enthusiasm for creating jewelry has been the inspiration of my career.

This book is dedicated to all those men and women who work long hours to make the silver and gold components that we designers have the great pleasure and privilege of arranging into finished jewelry.

ABOUT THE AUTHOR

Nancy Alden Wall (who writes and designs under the name Nancy Alden) is a jewelry designer and cofounder of the Beadworks Group, one of world's largest retailers of beads. As Beadworks' principal buyer and designer, she travels the world in search of the most beautiful components for jewelry design. She is as at home with gemstone merchants in Jaipur, silver makers in Bali, and glass artists in Bohemia as she is with pearl producers in China. Her knowledge of beads and findings is unrivalled, spanning all categories of material and all stages of production from the creation of a single bead to its final role in a finished piece of jewelry.

Starting as a silver and goldsmith, Nancy turned to designing with beads because of the vastly greater possibilities for creative expression. Having seen the world of jewelry design open for herself, she then went on to introduce other people to the creative pleasures and the economies of making their own jewelry. By creating Beadworks' classes and sharing her skills with other instructors, she has generated a network of teachers who have added to the ever-growing number of women and men able to design and create jewelry. Now, for the first time, she shares her design and production techniques in a comprehensive and easy-to-follow guide, enabling an even wider audience to make their own attractive necklaces, earrings, and bracelets. When she is not in search of new beads, Nancy divides her time between her home in Connecticut and her studio retreats in Europe and the Grenadines.

ABOUT BEADWORKS

In 1978, a small store in London began selling a very ancient product in a very novel way. Although beads are among the very earliest of traded articles, the concept of offering a large, sophisticated, and open display to the general public was new.

The shop never advertised—indeed, it didn't even have a name for many years—but the demand for its products was immediate and overwhelming. Simply by word of mouth, the original store became world famous.

With American jewelry designer Nancy Alden Wall, the concept expanded to North America, where it has grown to half a dozen stores and a mail order business. Beadworks has inspired people from around the world to open their own bead stores, enabling hundreds of thousands of people to make their own jewelry. You can visit Beadworks online at www.beadworks.com.

INDEX